BRIGHT NOTES

THE VICAR OF WAKEFIELD BY OLIVER GOLDSMITH

Intelligent Education

Nashville, Tennessee

BRIGHT NOTES: The Vicar of Wakefield
www.BrightNotes.com

No part of this publication may be used or reproduced in any manner whatsoever without written permission, except in the case of brief quotations in critical articles and reviews. For permissions, contact Influence Publishers http://www.influencepublishers.com.

ISBN: 978-1-645423-60-7 (Paperback)
ISBN: 978-1-645423-61-4 (eBook)

Published in accordance with the U.S. Copyright Office Orphan Works and Mass Digitization report of the register of copyrights, June 2015.

Originally published by Monarch Press.
James J. Greene; Gregor Roy, 1965
2020 Edition published by Influence Publishers.

Interior design by Lapiz Digital Services. Cover Design by Thinkpen Designs.

Printed in the United States of America.

Library of Congress Cataloging-in-Publication Data forthcoming.
Names: Intelligent Education
Title: BRIGHT NOTES: The Vicar of Wakefield
Subject: STU004000 STUDY AIDS / Book Notes

CONTENTS

1) Introduction to Oliver Goldsmith — 1

2) Introduction: Literary Trends and Personalities of the Eighteenth Century — 6

3) Introduction: A Survey of Augustan Prose: Essay, Satire and Novel — 14

4) Introduction to Vicar of Wakefield — 31

5) General Plot Outline — 44

6) Textual Analysis — 49
   - Chapters 1 - 8 — 49
   - Chapters 9 - 18 — 80
   - Chapters 25 - 32 — 97

7) Character Analyses — 108

8) Critical Commentary — 114

9) Essay Questions and Answers — 121

10) Bibliography — 125

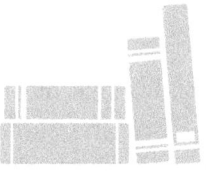

INTRODUCTION TO OLIVER GOLDSMITH

GOLDSMITH'S EARLY LIFE

Oliver Goldsmith's family was of English origin, but had long been settled in Ireland, where the writer was born on November 10, 1728. His father was a clergyman who also worked as a farmer, and Oliver was one of a large family. A good sketch of his father's character is given in Goldsmith's *The Citizen of the World*. It was said that the whole family was "generous, credulous, simple" and lacking in foresight or thrift. The writer spent a great part of his boyhood in the village of Lissoy where he received a sound though somewhat irregular education. In 1744 he entered Trinity College, Dublin, as a poor scholar – called in those days a "sizar" - and this poverty-stricken position caused the sensitive youth considerable humiliation. His unhappiness at college was increased by the fact that his tutor, who happened to be rather a brutal person, insisted on teaching logic and mathematics, both of which Goldsmith hated. The young man had a serious handicap in his appearance. He was gawky, awkward, and ungainly. He also continually broke college rules, which by no means helped his academic career. Despite these drawbacks, however, Goldsmith succeeded in obtaining a B. A. in 1749. His family had been pressing him for some time to become a clergyman, and he even prepared himself for this profession. When he went for his first interview with Bishop Synge of Elphin, however, he wore a pair of flaming scarlet breeches and was rejected as being a positive risk. He then spent some time looking around for a suitable career, but Goldsmith in this period showed himself to be an irresponsible spendthrift, squandering money which his relatives and widowed mother badly needed.

GOLDSMITH'S LATER LIFE

Early in 1753 he went to Edinburgh, the capital of Scotland, to study medicine. He was not a very industrious student, however, and attended only a few lectures before proceeding to Leyden, in Holland, where he continued his studies. From there he set out to do a walking tour of Europe "with one shirt in his pocket and a devout reliance on Providence," as Sir Walter Scott said. He crossed Flanders, France, Germany, Switzerland and Italy on foot, earning his keep at odd jobs as he went. During his travels he picked up considerable information which he later used in his books. He also claimed to have earned a medical degree at either Louvain or Padua. (One of Goldsmith's friends said later that he was forced to leave the Continent, since he killed more patients than he cured.) He returned to London early in 1756, where he lived a wretched, poverty-stricken existence, making ends meet by working at various menial occupations. By 1760 he had started hack-writing for booksellers, and in his *Present State of Polite Learning in Europe* he makes the following comments on this way of life: "The author, when unpatronized by the Great, has naturally recourse to the bookseller. There cannot be, perhaps, imagined a combination more prejudicial to taste than this. It is the interest of one to allow as little for writings, and of the other to write as much, as possible; accordingly, tedious compilations, and periodical magazines, are the result of their joint endeavors. In these circumstances, the author bids adieu to fame, writes for bread, and for that only. Imagination is seldom called in; he sits down to address the venal muse with the most phlegmatic apathy." This soul-destroying, penny-pinching existence, helped along by Goldsmith's reckless generosity and taste for extravagant clothes, led to a complete breakdown in his health. He died, wretchedly impoverished, on April 4, 1774, and was buried in Westminster Abbey.

GOLDSMITH'S MINOR WORKS

Much that Goldsmith wrote was hack work of no lasting literary merit and has naturally perished with his age. Yet the booksellers of his day found him a profitable writer, since he was industrious and wrote with an easy, flowing style. In fact, his natural talent as a stylist prompted the great Dr. Samuel Johnson to write in his **epitaph** that Goldsmith adorned every branch of literature that he touched. Among his lesser known works, he wrote histories of Rome, Greece and England, an English grammar, *A History of the Earth and Animated Nature, a History of Mecklenburgh*, and many other pieces which are no longer available. Dr. Johnson said of his *Animated Nature*: "He is now writing a Natural History, and will make it as interesting as a Persian tale." Goldsmith himself was acutely aware of the menial nature of his work, and admitted that in compiling one work called *Selections of English Poetry*, for example, he merely marked his selected passages with a red pencil. He counteracted his guilty feelings about accepting 200 pounds for this by claiming that "a man shows his judgment in these selections, and he may be often twenty years of his life cultivating that judgment." In the last years of his life, Goldsmith actually made good money - as much as 800 pounds a year - but he could never control his extravagance. His debts rose in proportion to his income, and at the time of his death he owed more than 2,000 pounds. Regarding Goldsmith's spending habits, Dr. Johnson remarked once: "Was ever poet so trusted before?"

GOLDSMITH'S MAJOR WORKS

Goldsmith is remembered for having written a variety of important works, including a book of essays (*The Citizen of the World*, 1760-61); a novel (*The Vicar of Wakefield*, 1766); and two plays (*The Good-Natured Man*, 1768, and *She Stoops to Conquer*, 1773). Of all the art forms he dealt with, he took greatest care with his poems, and we know for a fact that he took painstaking care with their composition and revision. He never revised *The Vicar of Wakefield*, however, although it was not published until a few years after he wrote it. Goldsmith said that there was no need to take further care with it, since he had already been paid for it. It is interesting to note that he never thought that he would enjoy a good reputation with posterity, and was continually depressed during his lifetime about lack of recognition. He need not have worried, however, since his works have enjoyed universal popularity right to the present day. He was uncouth personally, and wrote everything with a struggle. His resultant inferiority complex caused him to remark once that "the public will never do me justice; whenever I write anything, they make a point to know nothing about it." Yet his self-debasing attitude was really unjustified. He counted among his closest friends such eminent 18th Century figures as Dr. Samuel Johnson, the "Great Lexicographer"; Sir Joshua Reynolds, the painter; Edmund Burke, the orator; and David Garrick, the actor. He was also a privileged member of the exclusive Literary Club which used to meet every Monday night at a place called the Turk's Head in Soho, London. Also, most of his major works were hailed as soon as they were made public. *The Traveller*, for example, was described by Dr. Johnson as the finest poem written since the death of Alexander Pope. Within a mere five months, *The Vicar of Wakefield*, after a bad start, went into several editions. *The Deserted Village* and *She Stoops to Conquer* made him as renowned as Dr. Johnson himself. Since his death as well, Goldsmith has on the whole enjoyed a good reputation, mainly because people do not consider his works as shallow and superficial as those of many other writers of the 18th Century. His works have warmth, a sense of humanity and charm, which are qualities not often associated with other great writers of the age, such as Johnson, Fielding or Pope. But before proceeding to analyze Goldsmith's literary merit, with particular reference to *The Vicar of Wakefield*, some comments should be made on the social, historical, and literary background of that period, which is generally referred to as the Augustan Age.

INTRODUCTION: LITERARY TRENDS AND PERSONALITIES OF THE EIGHTEENTH CENTURY

THE AUGUSTAN AGE: SOCIAL BACKGROUND

Goldsmith's works can best be judged and enjoyed if we understand something about the background of the 18th Century. This is often called the Augustan Age after the period of Latin literature which prevailed during the reign of the Emperor Augustus. This age roughly spans the years between about 1660 and 1780, but for the sake of convenience we usually refer to it as the "18th Century." It is an interesting time, particularly since it bridged the gap between the 17th Century, which was noted for its strict scholarship, and the 19th Century, which was marked by religious and scientific skepticism. In the Augustan Age there was a growing interest in man and his society, and in the self, which was an integral part of that society. The age has often been attacked, somewhat unfairly, as one in which only glossy decoration and shallow elegance were admired. Yet it must be said in its defense that all different aspects of life were examined and analyzed by Augustan writers, and that these writers regarded the whole of society as its audience. It should also be noted that this society was often satirized - as in Alexander Pope's great poem, *The Rape of the Lock* - and even attacked with some genuine bitterness, as in Oliver Goldsmith's social poem, *The Deserted Village*. When we compare such poems to works written previous to the 18th Century, such as Edmund Spenser's *Faerie Queene* or John Milton's *Paradise Lost*, we get the impression that these earlier poets wrote exclusively for a very limited, scholarly audience. One very bad feature of the Augustan Age, however, was the fact that a writer often had to rely on the generous influence and financial support of a private patron in order to survive. Finding a patron usually meant that an author had to degrade himself; and the famous 18th Century literary giant, Dr. Samuel Johnson, wrote a magnificent letter decrying the patronage system, to a certain Lord Chesterfield who had humiliated Johnson. On the other hand, one good aspect of patronage was the fact that the patron's interests were often wide, ranging from contemporary politics to classical literature. This afforded the writer a wider range of topics to deal with than he might have had otherwise. The printing press also gained prominence in this age; and the tremendous financial success of the publication of Alexander Pope's *Iliad* and *Odyssey* proved that a writer could survive comfortably without the support of a private patron. England in the 18th Century also enjoyed a healthy, expanding economy, and it was at this time that Lloyd's famous shipping agency and the Bank of England were founded. London, of course, was the home of civilized society in the Augustan Age, although exotic places and tastes were also admired, as is shown in Goldsmith's *The Citizen of the World* and *The Traveller*. In this period, truth, superior taste, good sense, elegance, and the moral law were all held in high esteem. It was the age of "neoclassicism," by which writers judged contemporary man in the light of the ancient classics; and of "humanism," whereby man had to fashioned himself according to the best of past cultures. All this was expressed in the literary tradition of the age.

AUGUSTAN LITERARY TRADITION

The main rule of this tradition was that man should "follow Nature." This meant that he had to obey the strict rules of literary judgment and cultural taste by which he could fulfill himself. To achieve this, a writer had to have a thorough knowledge of classical literature, and was obliged to follow a strict set of rules and regulations. For example, everything had to be written with "wit," which in those days meant a lucid, clever way of expressing ideas. In poetry, this was done by the technique of rhyming "heroic couplets," which received the name from the fact that it seemed the neatest method of voicing a lofty opinion with clarity, control, and ease. Goldsmith himself perfected this technique, and one of the best examples of the heroic **couplet** is found in his description of the parson in *The Deserted Village*:

> **A man he was to all the country dear,**
> **And passing rich on forty pounds a year.**

To the Augustans, art had to be subservient to Nature, but according to Alexander Pope, Nature had to be "methodized." The result of this was that something which seems artificial to us was perfectly "natural" to the 18th Century mind. A study of the picnic scene in Goldsmith's *Vicar of Wakefield*, for example, shows how this process of methodizing Nature affected scenic descriptions. In the 18th Century, society had to be examined according to the rules of Reason and Common Sense, and this led to the writing of such critical and satirical works as Pope's *The Rape of the Lock*, Swift's *Gulliver's Travels*, and Goldsmith's *The Deserted Village*. Some great prose was also written at this time, in the form of both essays and novels. Joseph Addison and Richard Steele were the leading essayists, and their contributions to the periodicals *The Tatler* and *The Spectator* established a tone and quality of style which are hard to equal. It was the age in which prose in general and the novel in particular came into their own as art forms, and we shall shortly discuss the works of such prose writers as Daniel Defoe, Samuel Richardson, Tobias Smollett, Henry Fielding and Laurence Sterne. Then we will examine Goldsmith's *Vicar of Wakefield* in great detail. Because of the accentuation on classical rules and regulations, however, there was a tendency toward too much stifling formalism in 18th Century writing, and this led in turn to a certain monotonous conformity. Yet to counteract this drawback, the strict literary demands made on an author led to a remarkably high degree of technical skill and disciplined clarity. Before embarking on a detailed examination of the novel, however, it is necessary to discuss briefly the social and literary club of which Goldsmith was a member, and which was led by the giant of the Augustan Age, Dr. Samuel Johnson.

DR. SAMUEL JOHNSON

Born on September 18, 1709, at Lichfield, Johnson was the precocious son of a bookseller in that small cathedral town. He was of little use to his father, however, since he spent most of his time reading books rather than selling them, until he eventually was admitted to Pembroke College, Oxford, as a Commoner. He then found employment as a journalist in Birmingham, but in 1737 he went to London to embark on his literary career. In 1744 he established his reputation with his *Life of Richard Savage*, and in 1749 his poem *The Vanity of Human Wishes* appeared. At this time he started his greatest project, the *Dictionary of the English Language*, which appeared on April 15, 1755, in two folio volumes. He also wrote many essays for the periodical the *Rambler*; but although his biographer James Boswell said that in these he showed himself to be "a majestick teacher of moral and religious wisdom," Johnson was in fact heavy-handed and dull as an essayist. Of his prose works, his allegorical story *Rasselas*, written in 1759, and his *Lives of the Poets*, written in 1777, are those which are still most widely read. We owe a great deal of our knowledge of Johnson to Boswell, whose writings bring to life not only the personality of the great man, but also the character of The Club of which Goldsmith was a member.

JOHNSON'S LITERARY CLUB

There were nine original members of The Club, which was founded in 1764 and which met for supper, usually on Monday evenings, in the Turk's Head tavern in Soho. Of these members, the most prominent were Johnson himself, Sir Joshua Reynolds, Edmund Burke, and Oliver Goldsmith. In 1779 it was given the formal title of The Literary Club, and its membership grew to thirty-five, taking in such prominent figures as David Garrick the actor, Adam Smith the economist, Edward Gibbon the historian, and James Boswell the biographer. Johnson was inevitably the center of the group, which he stimulated to discussion and controversy by the brilliance of his conversational powers. The most eminent writers of the group, apart from Dr. Johnson, were Sir Joshua Reynolds (1723-92), Adam Smith (1723-90), Edmund Burke (1729-97), Edward Gibbon (1737-94) and Oliver Goldsmith (1728-74). It is interesting to note that apart from Goldsmith, the other four were only incidentally men of letters since they had earned renown in other fields of activity: Reynolds as a painter, Smith as a teacher of political economy, Burke as a political intellectual, and Gibbon as a professional historian. Only Goldsmith made his living as a full-time writer, and it would perhaps be appropriate here if we outlined briefly the main literary contributions of these writers. The student will then have some idea of the type of writing and intellectual tone which formed the setting for Goldsmith's efforts.

REYNOLDS

His main work was the collection of addresses to the Royal Academy of Art known as his *Discourses*. In these he develops the theory that "implicit obedience to the rules of art" must be shown by students if they wished to achieve the Grand Style which Reynolds himself practiced in his portraits. He recognized the fact, however, that a literal, slavish following of regulations was not so important as a preservation of the spirit of the law. His ideas are outlined with an ease of style characteristic of the age, but it should be stressed that as a philosophy of art the *Discourses* promulgate the lack of passion and spontaneity which was also a feature of the Augustan Age.

SMITH

His famous work, published in 1776, was *An Inquiry Into the Nature and Causes of the Wealth of Nations*, which cannot be read purely for its literary value, despite the high standard of its prose. Its essential worth lies in the fact that it revolutionized political and economic thinking by expounding the theory that a country's labor is the mainspring of "all the necessaries and conveniences of life" which it consumes annually. This economic principle has had far-reaching effects which have ruled a great deal of political thinking right down to the present day.

BURKE

He was an orator and politician more than a writer, but he raised political oratory to an art in itself, and eventually expressed his views in writing. In his *Thoughts on the Cause of the Present Discontents* (1770), he blamed contemporary discontent on what he called "a faction ruling by the private inclinations of a Court, against the general sense of the people." His *Speech on American Taxation* (1777) criticizes the government for its refusal to repeal the tea duty on the colonies. In his *Reflections on the Revolution in France* (1790), he defends the English crown against the idea that a monarch can be dethroned by the people, proceeding to deplore the excesses of the French revolutionaries. His last most important work, *Letters on the Proposals for Peace with the Regicide Director of France* (1796-97), is a bitter attack on the Pitt administration for attempting to come to terms with the Jacobins.

GIBBON

His great work is *The Decline and Fall of the Roman Empire*, which was published in 1776, 1781 and 1788. It is undoubtedly the most monumental single work written in the 18th Century, and Gibbon succeeded in collecting, controlling, and unifying a vast quantity of historical data with astonishing clarity and vision. While it is not our function here to analyze or criticize Gibbon either as a historian or literary artist, it should be said that he captured in this work all the best traditions of the age in its tone, style, scope and analytical fervor.

GOLDSMITH

In many ways, the gawky, irresponsible, and charming Irishman was underestimated by most members of the Literary Club, and it was really Dr. Johnson who recognized and publicly lauded the man's talents. To begin with, his output was enormous and varied, and although much of it was hack-work, he approached even the most menial literary chore with a sense of dedication and artistic integrity worthy of the highest praise. Because of his obvious weaknesses as a person, however, he was an easy target for criticism, and according to Boswell, Johnson himself frequently flayed him verbally for his foibles. Even his stammering speech was an object of amusement for the group, as exemplified by the actor David Garrick's famous jibe that Goldsmith "wrote like an angel, but talk'd like poor Poll." We have already listed his major and minor works, some of which, particularly *The Vicar of Wakefield*, we shall be discussing later in some detail. All his works are stamped with an inimitable charm, and on occasion he displays a remarkable degree of satirical insight into the manners and mores of the times. At one time, for example, when he was working for a publisher of children's books called John Newbery, he devised the idea of writing some "Chinese letters" which were collected in 1762 into the book known as *The Citizen of the World*. In this work he makes pungent, amusing, and satirical comments on the Augustan way of life through the observations of a fictitious Chinese philosopher visiting London. This work also introduces us to two of Goldsmith's best-drawn characters Beau Tibbs and The Man in Black. Although his poems *The Traveller* and *The Deserted Village* are in some ways marred by the worst artificial features of the age, they are nevertheless refreshingly simple and emotionally honest. Our main concern, however, is with *The Vicar of Wakefield*, but to fully appreciate this work we must first look into the Augustan prose tradition in general and the background development of the novel in particular.

INTRODUCTION: A SURVEY OF AUGUSTAN PROSE: ESSAY, SATIRE AND NOVEL

THE ESSAY: ADDISON AND STEELE

One of the most interesting art forms that was developed in the Augustan Age was the essay, and the two writers who brought this form to a high standard of perfection were Joseph Addison and Richard Steele. Later imitators such as Johnson, Fielding, and Goldsmith continued to popularize the essay, but none of them quite succeeded in achieving the elegance of style and power of perception captured by these two masters. In the 19th Century, writers like De Quincey, Hazlitt and Lamb used the essay as a highly personal mode of self-expression. But in the early 18th Century, the essays of Addison and Steele were rather journalistic expressions of public taste and opinion, serving an important social function in the relative absence of newspapers. Historically, the scene was set for the essayist because of the ecclesiastical, social and political turmoil existing in England in the latter half of the 17th Century. Steele and Addison brought a cohesion to this world with their urbane wit, sense of moral decency, and balanced reason, all expressed in superb prose. A brief comment on the background of each essayist will give the student a fuller appreciation of their joint contribution to the art of the essay.

Richard Steele

Born in Dublin in 1672, Steele attended Oxford University for a time, but left to become a soldier. As a private, junior officer, and captain, he learned a great deal about the raw side of human nature, and this education stood him in good stead when he came to write for the *Tatler* periodical, which he founded. In 1701 he wrote his first book, *The Christian Hero*, but no one seemed impressed by the moral ideas expressed in it, so he went on to writing plays. One of these dramatic efforts, *The Conscious Lovers*, was so successful that he was given the political appointment of Gazetteer and Gentleman Usher at Court.

Joseph Addison

Addison had more of a cultured, cosmopolitan background than Steele, and after spending ten years at Magdalen College, Oxford, he began writing poems in both English and Latin. Even the great poet Dryden was so impressed by these that he referred to him as "the most ingenious J. Addison of Oxford," and his future seemed assured. He was granted a traveling scholarship of 300 pounds a year which enabled him to visit France, Italy, Germany and Holland. At this time he wrote a poem called *The Campaign* which was politically pleasing to the political party known as the Whigs, who appointed him Under-Secretary of State. It was at this time, 1709, that Steele's *Tatler* appeared, and Addison, recognizing its literary merit, offered his services as a contributor.

The Tatler

The first issue of the periodical appeared on April 12, 1709. Steele wished to remain anonymous, and used the pseudonym Isaac Bickerstaff to compose his essays. At first his essays concerned the activities of the London coffee houses, which were the centers of literary discussions, political controversies, and social gossip. The periodical was immediately successful, appearing three times a week on Tuesdays, Thursdays and Saturdays. Although Addison wrote some of his most charming essays in the *Tatler*, it was Steele who really established its moral tone, guiding public taste in so doing. Steele himself stated that by founding the periodical, he wished to "expose the false arts of life, to pull off the disguises of cunning, vanity, and affectation, and to recommend a general simplicity in our dress, our discourse, and our behaviour." Unfortunately, Steele began to concentrate too much on political matters, which elicited such official disfavor that he lost his honored position as Gazetteer. Addison at this time gave some prudent advice resulting in the termination of the *Tatler* and the foundation of a new, non-political journal called the *Spectator*.

The Spectator

This periodical first appeared in March, 1711. It was a completely joint enterprise by Addison and Steele, running to a total of 555 numbers. In this case, it was Addison who outlined the aims of the journal when he wrote: "It was said of Socrates that he brought philosophy down from heaven to inhabit among men; and I shall be ambitious to have it said of me that I have brought philosophy out of closets and libraries, schools, colleges, to dwell in clubs and assemblies, at tea-tables and in coffee-houses." In the *Spectator*, Addison brought the essay as an art form to a high standard of clarity and perception. They brought a rich comic flavor to prose with the "Sir Roger de Coverley" series, and one of the remarkable features of their essays is the way in which they introduced to them all the best features of other art forms. Their style was unique, inasmuch as they brought an element of colloquialism to prose, which makes many of the *Spectator* pieces sound like speech itself. On the whole, it can be said that Addison and Steele together elevated the tone of Augustan prose, establishing a tradition of elegance, clarity, and wit to which Goldsmith fell heir by the time he came to write *The Vicar of Wakefield*.

SATIRE: JONATHAN SWIFT

Born in Dublin of English parents and educated at Trinity College, Dublin, Dean Swift is probably the greatest satirist in English literature. The great critic George Saintsbury said of him that "If intellectual genius and literary art be taken together, no prose-writer, who is a prose-writer mainly, is Swift's superior, and a man might be hard put to it to say who among such writers in the plainer English can be pronounced his equal." Plagued by bodily ailments, he was a thoroughgoing misanthrope who detested mankind with a raging indignation probably unequalled in the history of literature. Yet he was able to express this contempt for mankind's cruelties and hypocrisies in superb prose, and his *Tale of a Tub* and *Gulliver's Travels* stand as two of the world's great satirical masterpieces. In *Gulliver's Travels* he expresses all the bitterness, venom and despair which he felt personally at mankind's inadequacies. It is rather ironical that one of the most vitriolic attacks on humanity has survived as a fairy tale read with delight by the young and innocent. But it must be remembered that it is in fact a ruthless satire, not only on men, but on the traditional type of exotic travelers' tales so popular in Swift's day. Gulliver's life, use of maps, adventures, and so on are all outlined brilliantly within the framework of a scientific fantasy which veils the biting nature of the **satire**. Each portion of the book attacks the human race from an entirely different angle. Swift's *Tale of a Tub*, although much less widely read, is probably his best work from a purely literary point of view. The title is taken from the ancient myth that if a ship's crew threw a tub to a school of whales, they would play with it and leave the ship alone. The work begins with a humorous invocation to "Prince Posterity," followed by a mock-serious discussion of oratorical machines and customs of Grub Street. Swift then plunges into the satirical core of the work, telling us of the father who dies, bequeathing his goods to his three sons, Peter, Martin, and Jack, symbolizing the Roman Catholic Church, the Church of England, and Dissent respectively. Of this work Swift himself exclaimed, "Good God, what a genius I was when I wrote that Book!" It has been said of Swift that he brought both disgrace and honor to literature, since he reaches the lowest depths possible in voicing his loathing for humanity, yet elevated **satire** to almost unsurpassed heights of wit and perception. His contribution to the development of English prose is outstanding, and helps form the background against which Goldsmith wrote his famous novel.

THE NOVEL: GENERAL COMMENTS

The *Oxford Dictionary* tells us that a novel is "A fictitious prose narrative of considerable length, in which characters and actions representative of real life are portrayed in a plot of more or less complexity." This definition can not only be expanded, but can also be repudiated to a certain extent, inasmuch as many novels are not purely imaginative works, but get their sources from real life events. It is also not quite true that the fictional aspects of all novels are "representative of real life," and many writers have deliberately violated this precept in order to achieve some particular desired effect. Even the concept of a plot can be called in question, since some novelists concentrate on developing a situation without the "beginning, middle and end" idea of the traditional plot novel. Some critics, of course, say that such a work cannot really be placed in the historical context of the novel. This argument can be refuted, however, by reference to such a novelist as Laurence Sterne, to whom plot was of no consequence, and who gave free rein to forming fantastic thoughts and developing fanciful ideas by his unique use of language. It is, in fact, impossible to give one definition of the novel which is all-embracing. There have even been novels written in verse form - Geoffrey Chaucer's *Troilus and Criseyde* is a good example - as well as novels of biography, politics, sociology, history, religion, philosophy, psychology, and sentiment. The novel of sentiment is exemplified by Oliver Goldsmith's *The Vicar of Wakefield*, which we will be studying shortly in great detail. There are even some novels, such as James Joyce's *Finnegans Wake*, which defy any classification. In the Augustan Age, however, there were clear-cut lines along which the novel developed. By examining briefly the works and art of Daniel Defoe, Samuel Richardson, Henry Fielding, Laurence Sterne, Tobias Smollet and Jane Austen, the student will have a firm foundation upon which to base his detailed study of *The Vicar of Wakefield*. Before we do this, however, it would be appropriate to take a backward glance at the history of the English novel during Elizabethan times, since it was from this early tradition that the novelists of the Augustan Age, including Goldsmith, received the basis of their art.

THE ELIZABETHAN NOVEL

There were two aspects of the Elizabethan novel, one leaning toward rather sordid social **realism**, and the other toward an idyllic, non-realistic vision of pastoral romance. We must not forget, however, that Elizabethan novelists were not used to writing prose, and were working under the decided disadvantage of having no great prose heritage to fall back on. On reading some Elizabethan novels, one often gets the impression that they would have been more successful as poems or plays. We must not fall into the trap of being too disparaging of them, however, since they were pioneering efforts which led to the future, flourishing era of the great English novel. There were five major Elizabethan novelists, whose works we will outline briefly as a stepping stone to our general survey of the 18th Century novel and precise examination of Goldsmith's novel.

John Lyly

His two major novels were *Euphues, The Anatomy of Wit* (1578) and *Euphues and his England* (1580). Although the plot and **theme** of these two works are simple, they are inflated and swollen beyond all proportion in a bloated, turgid style packed with tedious moralizing. This ornate, unnatural style, which actually became known as "euphuism," was highly acceptable to Elizabethans, who were prone to admiring the long-winded French, Spanish and Italian prose romances of the day. Yet although this artificial, intricate style is unpalatable to modern readers, it did represent a genuine attempt on Lyly's part to weave clarity, ornament, elegance, and classical learning into one comprehensively balanced tapestry.

Sir Philip Sidney

Sidney's *The Countesse of Pembrokes Arcadia* was first published in 1590, although the author had died a few years earlier. The *Arcadia* was actually written for Sidney's sister, but its literary merit is not very high. From the stylistic point of view, however, it does contain some passages of pastoral charm, and the following brief extract will give the student some idea of the type of prose which was fashionable in Elizabethan literary circles: "There were hilles which garnished their proud heights with stately trees; humble valleis, whose base estate seemed comforted with the refreshing of silver rivers; meadows, enameld with al sorts of eypleasing floures; thickets, which being lined with most precious shade, were witnessed so to by the chereful desposition of many wel-tuned birds."

Thomas Lodge

The title of Lodge's most famous work, *Rosalynde; Euphues' Golden Legacie*, shows immediately the author's debt to Lyly. Only the style of *Rosalynde* is euphuiistic, however, because Lodge was influenced in the **theme** of his novel by pastoral Greek romances. As a matter of fact, Elizabethan novels were influenced greatly by the Greek classical atmosphere, and this erotic innocence and sylvan beauty of tone affected prose fiction right through the Augustan Age. The student should bear this in mind when he reads *The Vicar of Wakefield*, where this pastoral, idyllic aura is very much in evidence.

Thomas Nashe

Nashe's principal work is called *The Unfortunate Traveller, or The Life of Jacke Wilton*, and with this novel we leave the world of pastoral charm and enter the ugly domain of lust, horror, and crime. In one sense it can be described as the first English historical novel, inasmuch as renowned contemporary figures keep appearing on its pages: Erasmus, the Earl of Surrey, and Sir Thomas More, for example, all find their way somehow into this roistering, Rabelaisian tale. It has also been described as the first real English picaresque novel, which is a type of novel dealing with clever vagabonds and their scandalous adventures. Nashe wrote torrents of words, and his style has been described as a mixture of that of James Joyce and Rabelais. It is also an interesting novel from the point of view of characterization, inasmuch as a wide social range is represented, although with such exaggeration that it can hardly be described as a "realistic" work.

Thomas Deloney

Unlike the above writers, Deloney was not university educated, but was a tradesman and writer of ballads. When he eventually turned to novel writing, it was with the deliberate intention of introducing a more democratic tone to literature by revealing the lives of such people as spinners, weavers, and shoemakers. His three main novels are *Jacke of Newbury* (1597), *Thomas of Reading* (1600), and *The Gentle Craft* (1597-98), but they are on the whole unsuccessful due to loose construction, lack of unity, and episodic unevenness. Yet his contribution to the history of the English novel is an important one, inasmuch as he did succeed in demonstrating the fact that pastoral elegance and artificial sentiment were not essential to the art of the novel.

From a linguistic point of view as well, Deloney wrote in a lucid, straightforward style which is a refreshing change from the ornate extravagances of some of his contemporaries.

THE RISE OF THE AUGUSTAN NOVEL

Before we discuss the main contribution of Oliver Goldsmith to the art of the novel by embarking on a detailed analysis of *The Vicar of Wakefield*, the student should be aware of the types of novel that arose and developed throughout the 18th Century. It will then be more interesting to study Goldsmith's work in the light of what we have learned, and to examine the possible categories into which it could be placed. In a very real sense, Augustan prose brought the novel as an art form into the permanent domain of great literature. Its tremendous growth and universal acceptance can be compared to the flourishing of the drama in Elizabethan times or the flowering of spiritual poetry in the 17th Century. As we have seen, fiction was not an 18th Century invention. Prior to the Elizabethan Age, which we have discussed very briefly, there was an abundance of legends, myths, and invented prose narratives in the Middle Ages. The Renaissance period itself abounded in pastoral romances, classical prose translations, and allegories. Then a new trend appeared whereby fiction was on the whole divorced from the realities of life, taking the form of moral narratives and satires. Three main demands were made, in fact, in order that fiction might survive and develop into the full-fledged literary form known as the novel:

1. The prose with which the plot, **theme**, ideas and characters of the novel were expressed had to be credible, readable, and reliable.

2. There had to be a guarantee of enough readers to appreciate this unique brand of narrative and to show a willingness to help sponsor its development.

3. It was imperative that faith in the novel would ensure its survival and make it truly worthy of talented artistic endeavor.

These demands had certainly been met on the Continent through the successful literary endeavors of Rabelais and Cervantes, and even by the universal acceptance of the fashionable French romances. With respect to the English novel, however, it is interesting to note that in some ways it developed more by accident than by deliberately planned effort. Daniel Defoe, for example, more or less drifted from a biographical travel story into an imaginative narrative; Richardson started penning model letters and ended writing an epistolary narrative; Fielding's work was prompted as a reaction to Richardson's prudish moralizing. We will include Jane Austen in our brief survey, since in many ways her novels "rounded off" the period of the Augustan novel and heralded the beginning of modern fiction. Goldsmith's *Vicar of Wakefield* will eventually be analyzed for its own intrinsic merit, and scrutinized in the light of the Augustan literary and historical context.

THE AUGUSTAN ACHIEVEMENT IN THE NOVEL

On the whole, the 18th Century novel was marked by a big, all-embracing plan, using genuine material from its society. The writer usually concentrated on either a short or a long stretch of his hero's life story, and often allowed a good deal of coincidence to influence the happenings of his story. The Augustan novelist was also prone to digress often from the central "spine" of the narrative. The most important innovation in this period was the comprehension and development of plot and character, employed on a cause-and-effect basis more than as mere episodic devices. There was nevertheless a certain unreality in many of the Augustan novels, which we will discuss when we come to *The Vicar of Wakefield*; the disorganized events of Defoe and Smollet are in fact more true to life than the studied planning of, say, Richardson or Fielding. Yet the reader often prefers the unruly flux of daily life to be planned and organized in a novel, and this was particularly true in the context of 18th Century sensibility. We shall now examine six types of Augustan novel to give the student some idea of the growing diversity of this art form:

1. Fiction deliberately designed to pass as fact, exemplified by the works of Daniel Defoe.

2. Sentimental morality as expounded by Samuel Richardson.

3. Robust **realism**, developed in the works of Henry Fielding.

4. Humor, which we find in Laurence Sterne.

5. Journalistic adventure, captured in the writings of Tobias Smollett.

6. **Realism**, humor and personal commentary, found in the novels of Jane Austin.

Before commenting on each of these forms, however, we should make some comment on other 18th Century writers whose efforts helped to develop the art of the novel.

OTHER AUGUSTAN NOVELISTS

Apart from the above six writers and, of course, Goldsmith with whom we will shortly be dealing in detail, there were many other novelists of varying literary stature who are worthy of mention. In the category of portentous Gothic spine-chillers, for example, we have Horace Walpole's *Castle of Otranto* (1764). We have the ultra-sentimental pathos of Henry MacKenzie's *Man of Feeling* (1771). Richard Graves poked fun at Methodism with *The Spiritual Quixote* (1772). We have the grandiose meditations of Dr. Johnson's *Rasselas* (1759). There was the tremendously popular tale of vitality and youth, Fanny Burney's *Evelina* (1778). And finally, in the realm of exotic Oriental fantasy, there was Beckford's *Vathek* (1786). From this brief survey alone, the student can see how the novel was branching out into various experimental channels in the course of the 18th Century. We shall now comment briefly on the six types of novel outlined above.

Fiction Designed As Fact

This type of novel is best illustrated by Daniel Defoe's *Robinson Crusoe*, and in this respect the student should remember Charles Lamb's comment on Defoe's literary efforts: "It is impossible to believe, while you are reading them, that a real person is not narrating to you everywhere nothing but what really happened to himself." Defoe was a realist inasmuch as he made his people speak as they would in real life, and this **realism** is enhanced by the fact that most of his characters belong to the unsophisticated, unlettered class. Defoe's *Journal of the Plague Year* is another excellent example of his "invention of truth" - it is pure fiction, yet it was accepted as fact when it was published, and has even been quoted by historians as factual evidence. Actually, Defoe was only five when the Great Plague took place. While *Robinson Crusoe* can be categorized as one of the first attempts at realistic fiction, Defoe's *Memoirs of a Cavalier* is probably the first attempt at the historical novel, in which real and imaginary figures are introduced and intermingled.

Sentimental Morality

Samuel Richardson's novel *Pamela, or Virtue Rewarded*, in fact marks the real beginning of the English novel. It was written as a conscious attempt to preach a moral lesson and to protect the young and innocent, which prompted Dr. Johnson to remark that Richardson taught "the passions to move at the command of virtue." *Pamela* is the story of an innocent, virtuous young girl who is almost led down the path of destruction by her sinister master, but whose high standard of morality wins out in the end. This novel was followed in 1748 by another called *Clarissa, or the Adventures of a Young Lady*. It is in one way quite amazing that *Clarissa*, which, with *Pamela*, is a maudlin, mawkishly sentimental piece of literary rubbish, was hailed in England and throughout Europe as a masterpiece. Yet both *Pamela* and *Clarissa* are tremendously important works in the history of the novel. They were written mainly for an audience of women, and were tremendously democratic by 18th Century standards, inasmuch as a servant girl is the heroine. The famous 18th Century philosopher, Denis Diderot, put Richardson in the same category as Homer and Euripides, and Rousseau's *La Nouvelle Héloïse* is modeled after *Clarissa*.

Robust Realism

While Richardson is credited with inventing the English novel, Henry Fielding must be honored for elevating it to a standard of vigorous **realism** and healthy inventiveness. Fielding wrote his first novel, *Joseph Andrews*, as a **burlesque** of Richardson's *Pamela* by transferring all the heroine's virtues and plights to her brother. The most remarkable feature of the book, however, is the masterly portrayal of the odd, simple, and lovable Parson Adams, whom certain critics say Goldsmith had in mind to some extent when he wrote *The Vicar of Wakefield*. Fielding's masterpiece, however, is *Tom Jones, or the History of a Foundling*, which was published in 1749, and it still stands as one of the greatest works in English literature. Its characters are credible, endearing, and thoroughly realistic, and the critic Hazlitt was not exaggerating when he said of Fielding: "As a painter of real life he was equal to Hogarth; as a mere observer of human nature, he was little inferior to Shakespeare."

Humor

The Augustan novel of humor is best exemplified by Laurence Sterne's *Tristram Shandy*, first published in 1759. Although it is not exactly a narrative in the true sense of the word, its loosely strung fiction contains an immortal and brilliantly drawn character in the person of Uncle Toby. Hazlitt said that Uncle Toby is "one of the finest compliments ever paid to human nature," and Thomas Carlyle compares Sterne to Cervantes. There is nevertheless a great deal of coarseness and vulgarity in the novel itself, which is explained not only by the coarseness of the age but also by the warped personality of Sterne himself. Samuel Taylor Coleridge said that Sterne should be blamed for "using the best dispositions of our nature as the panders and condiments for the basest." Despite these criticisms, however, *Tristram Shandy* stands as an outstanding work of humor and characterization because of the masterly portrayal of Uncle Toby.

Journalistic Adventure

This type of 18th Century novel found its master in Tobias Smollett, whose most famous works are *The Adventures of Roderick Random* (1748), *The Adventures of Peregrine Pickle* (1749), and *The Expedition of Humphrey Clinker* (1771). *Roderick Random* is a loosely knit string of adventures, largely autobiographical, which ends up as a robust, mobile adventure yam. *Peregrine Pickle* is an interesting work inasmuch as Smollett introduced two characters who have nothing to do with the story, purely for journalistic effect. *Humphrey Clinker* is generally considered to be the best of his novels, of which Thackeray comments: "*Humphrey Clinker* is, I do think, the most laughable story that has ever been written since the goodly art of novel-writing began." Smollett's great contribution to the Augustan novel was, in fact, his ability to fuse journalism, adventure, and fiction into a cohesive and comprehensible whole.

Realism, Humor And Personal Commentary

Jane Austen succeeded in combining these three qualities with a delicacy of detail and accuracy of perception which make her works outstanding. In her novels *Sense and Sensibility, Pride and Prejudice, Mansfield Park*, and *Emma*, she deals with the neighborly aspects of family life, though there is an inevitable vein of class distinction running through them all. One cannot help being aware that democratic principles were still alien to Jane Austen's conception of society, but we must remember that her view of life was a restricted and highly personal one. And in depicting this mode of life, she is unparalleled for her sense of comedy and **realism**. George Saintsbury summed up her contribution to the history of the English novel when he wrote: "Simple as are the plots, they are worked out with extraordinary closeness and completeness, and the characters and dialogue are of such astonishing finesse and life that it would hardly matter if there were no plot at all. From first to last this hold on life never fails Miss Austen, nor does the simple, suggestive, half-ironic style in which she manages to convey her meaning."

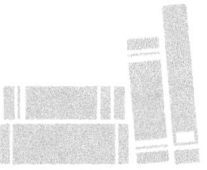

INTRODUCTION TO VICAR OF WAKEFIELD

PUBLICATION

In 1766, in the journal called *St. James's Chronicle*, the following advertisement appeared: "In a few days will be published in two volumes, twelves, price six shillings bound, or five shillings sewed, the *Vicar of Wakefield*. A tale, supposed to be written by himself. Printed for F. Newbery at the Crown in Paternoster Row." This announcement would not be particularly surprising were it not for the fact that the manuscript of Goldsmith's novel had already been in the hands of the publisher for almost two years. Dr. Johnson reputedly suggested that Newbery withhold publication until Goldsmith's reputation had been established with the success of his poem *The Traveller*, which had gone into its fourth edition after first appearing in 1764. In any case, from the time he wrote it in 1762 until the date of its publication, Goldsmith did nothing to retouch the work. The reason for this unwillingness to improve the novel was given by Goldsmith himself to a certain Dr. Farr. The writer said to the doctor: "He [Newbery] gave me 60 pounds for the copy; and had I made it ever so perfect or correct, I should not have had a shilling more." Another version of the transaction, according to James Boswell, is that Dr. Johnson arranged the sale of the book in 1762 in order to prevent Goldsmith's imprisonment for debt.

ASPECTS OF THE NOVEL

The Vicar of Wakefield is still widely read, particularly in high schools, and the very fact that it has survived so long is testimony enough to a certain literary merit. Many varied opinions have been expressed on its value, however, and it would be useful for the student to be made aware of several points of view so that he can reach his own conclusion.

Some Inconsistencies

The Vicar of Wakefield is essentially the work on which Goldsmith's reputation as a writer rests. It was tremendously successful in his own day, and still enjoys a wide popularity. Although a great deal of stoicism and a sense of resignation are lauded throughout the book, it contains many flaws which make its survival a source of some surprise to certain critics There is, for example, too much "goodness" displayed, which prevents the novel from being entirely satisfactory. The sweetness of nature and naivete of character on the part of the vicar and his family are too incredible. Throughout the novel there is also a lack of poise which Goldsmith displays in the rest of his major works. For one thing, it is too short to allow for complete development of plot, **theme**, and character; and the tremendous onslaught of disastrous events at the end of the story seems totally forced and unreal. When the vicar, in jail, learns that one daughter has died and another has been abducted by ruffians, his increased resignation is unnatural. Again, the very idea of the vicar's delivering a sermon on the "equal dealings of providence" is almost ludicrous in context. The sermon, moreover, is thoroughly tedious. Probably the novel fails because of Goldsmith's uneasy and ambiguous attitude toward the vicar himself. It would seem that the vicar's character would lend itself naturally to the gently ironical touch of which Goldsmith was capable. But he chose to write the novel in the first person, so that we are often unsure as to whether he meant to be ironical or not. The sermon we have just mentioned, for example, is boring if taken seriously, but could have been amusing if Goldsmith had made his intention clear. The vicar is also made to appear extremely prudish, as in the scene when he finds his daughters dressed for church in what he calls "frippery." His smug comment that "the nakedness of the indigent world may be clothed from the trimmings of the vain" seems to call for some kind of critical commentary from Goldsmith, but none is forthcoming. There is, moreover, a solemnity about the tone which seems out of keeping with Goldsmith's character.

The Novel And Augustan Sensibility

Another criticism leveled against the work is that it contains some of the shallowest, most artificial features of Augustan sensibility. We mentioned earlier Alexander Pope's dictum that Nature in the 18th Century sense of the word should be "methodized" in order to make it more beautiful. A good example of this artificially imposed embellishment of natural scenic beauty is contained in the scene in which the vicar and his family go on a picnic. Goldsmith's description of the idyllic scene speaks for itself:

> On these occasions, our two little ones always read for us, and they were regularly served after we were done. Sometimes, to give a variety to our amusements, the girls sung to the guitar; and while they thus formed a little concert, my wife and I would stroll down the sloping field, that was embellished with blue-bells and centaury, talk of our children

with rapture, and enjoy the breeze that wafted both health and harmony.

The vicar himself described this scene as "vacant hilarity," but even the most unimaginative reader cannot help being aware of the total artificiality of the setting. Nature has in fact been "dolled up" here to suit the occasion.

Some Minor Flaws

A careful examination of the text exposes some minor flaws in Goldsmith's writing which he would have undoubtedly caught had he revised his work carefully. We are told, for example, that the concert which takes place during the picnic scene is a novelty for such an occasion, that it adds "variety" to the scene. Only a few lines later, however, we are informed that "our young musicians began their usual concert" (author's italics), showing a certain lack of consistency on Goldsmith's part. Such carelessness certainly does not help to enhance the general picture. The author's choice of language too is often embarrassingly weak and inept, and his continual use of such words as "wafted" and "rapture" adds an unnatural air of coyness and sweetness to his descriptions. His minor characterization is also inadequate in certain respects. The vicar's daughters, for example, seem pretty much identical, so much so that the reader often has to keep looking back to their initial introduction in order to find out which one is which. Goldsmith often fails to grip us emotionally, as in the scene where the vicar and his wife are grief-stricken at their daughters' abduction. Critics of the novel feel quite simply that Goldsmith failed completely to attain any emotional rapport between his readers and his characters. His central participants are too generally drawn, with no subjectivity or inner life. These critics say that, at best, *The Vicar of Wakefield* is a flimsy and slender literary creation.

A Defense Of The Novel

Champions of *The Vicar of Wakefield* claim that with this work Goldsmith brought a sense of charm to the novel which has been enjoyed by two centuries of readers. It is held that children to whom the book is read are inevitably charmed and excited by it. The novel has many varied levels of meaning, and if approached in the spirit of Coleridge's "willing suspension of disbelief," the reader can easily forgive such license as Goldsmith's use of coincidence. There are periodic surprises throughout the novel, and the reader's curiosity is continually aroused, while the author quietly and subtly assures us that everything will be resolved in the end. It should be read first and foremost as a good, simple story. Some people have complained that the novel is sentimental. To this objection it could be answered that there is more nobility than sentimentality about a father who wholeheartedly loves his family and shows grief over his daughter's falling prey to an unscrupulous seducer. It should be remembered, furthermore, that Goldsmith himself hated cheap sentimentality. While it is true that Dr. Primrose, the vicar, is often caught unawares by selfish swindlers, this could well be regarded as the endearing quality of a simple, trusting person.

Humor In The Novel

Those who defend the work claim that it contains a great deal of humor which often goes unappreciated. While we may laugh at Dr. Primrose's foibles, it is with sympathy rather than contempt.

He is a very simple man in many ways, but it is an admirable brand of simplicity born of religious faith and trust in mankind. His keen perception into the vain pretentiousness of his own family causes us to laugh with him when his good sense and integrity prevail. It has been pointed out that if anyone imagines Dr. Primrose to be a fool worthy only of mockery, let him read the opening sentence of the novel and let him ponder: "I was ever of opinion, that the honest man who married and brought up a large family, did more service than he who continued single and only talked of population." It should be remembered too that Dr. Primrose is a fictitious character through whom Goldsmith displays many traits with **irony** and **satire**. Some critics have tried to compare Dr. Primrose to Chaucer's parson, but this comparison is invalid: Chaucer's prelate is a seriously drawn character, while Goldsmith's is a serious character with laughable flaws and endearing foibles. Dr. Primrose is much more akin in spirit to Fielding's Parson Adams, both being endowed with qualities of charm, courage and innocence which make them lovable and delightfully amusing. Yet throughout all the humor, Goldsmith succeeds in interposing many serious notes. Dr. Primrose - and, of course, Goldsmith himself - had strong views on serious topics such as debtors' prisons and penal reform. It has been said that in this novel Goldsmith's voice was on the side of the angels.

General Aspects

It is almost certain that Goldsmith learned a great deal from Fielding, not only in his ideas on social reform and humanitarian attitudes, but also in his use of subtle wit. He also undoubtedly learned a great deal from Fielding about the hard craft of constructing a good, solid story. It has been claimed that *The Vicar of Wakefield* is more cohesive and less episodic than *Joseph*

Andrews, yet not so intricately designed as *Tom Jones*. The reader should also bear in mind that apart from Squire Thornhill, who is an out-and-out scoundrel, all the characters are drawn at different levels of **satire** except the son, George, who represents Goldsmith himself. Another delightful aspect of the book is the clever way in which the novelist introduces ballads, **burlesques** and lyrics, such as the "**Elegy** on the Death of a Mad Dog," the song of Edwin and Angelina, and the well-known poem, "When Lovely Woman Stoops to Folly." All these minor elements must be taken into consideration in our appraisal of the novel, not forgetting the fact that Goldsmith shares with Addison, Fielding, and Gibbon the distinction of being one of the masters of elegant prose. Although he may have "talked like poor Poll," to quote Garrick, he certainly "wrote like an angel," with clarity, perception, and wit.

Goldsmith's Prose

This has not been appreciated enough by modern readers of his novel. His use of antithesis and other verbal techniques, for example, enhances his style and raises the general tone of his narrative. For example, in the scene where the Vicar's daughters are about to meet the Squire, the reader is told that there was hardly a farmer's daughter within a ten-mile radius "but what had found him successful and faithless." In spite of this, the daughters seem delighted at the possibility of making a conquest, nor is their mother "less pleased and confident of their allurements and virtue." Note also the elegance of **diction** in the Vicar's sermon to the prisoners, particularly when he talks of "those shackles, that tyranny has imposed or crime made necessary"; or when he proceeds with "O my friends, what a glorious exchange would heaven be for these! To fly through regions unconfined as air, to bask in the sunshine of eternal bliss, to carrol over endless hymns of praise, to have no master to threaten or insult us, but the form of Goodness himself for ever in our eyes; when I think of these things, death becomes the messenger of very glad tidings; when I think of these things, his sharpest arrow becomes the staff of my support; when I think of these things, what is there in life worth having? when I think of these things, what is there that should not be spurned away? Kings in their palaces should groan for such advantages; but we, humbled as we are, should yearn for them." There is an appropriateness of feeling and control of judgment throughout this whole sermon which, contrasted as it is with the wretchedness of the surroundings, is an excellent example of the Augustan "set piece." Behind his smoothly controlled phrase, Goldsmith showed obvious pleasure in finding a neat definition to fit a situation. When he remarks on the system of patronage in France, for example, he says that the aristocracy had "a most pleasing way of satisfying the vanity of an author, without indulging his avarice." The prose masters of the Augustan Age were experts at controlling **diction**, embellishing the surface of their tale, and achieving the most appropriate turn of phrase. They had one advantage, however, inasmuch as the vocabulary of the age was solidly defined, making it easier for writers to describe situations and express emotions smoothly and precisely. Defenders of Goldsmith's novels point to the fact that he was a master of the craft of prose and captured in his book all the most pleasing elements of 18th Century diction.

Didactic Elements

The 18th Century has been called, among other things, the **Didactic** Age, which means that people in those days favored literature which taught lessons. In this respect it has been pointed out that the great appeal of *The Vicar of Wakefield* lies not in its charm, whimsy, or humor, but in its **didactic** elements. Somehow or other it succeeds in weaving its message into our habits of thought, while doing so on a purely domestic level. Considering the fact that Goldsmith encompassed the wide **didactic** aspects of his story in a restricted setting, this sets him apart from writers like Smollett, Fielding, and Richardson, who needed a much wider range of location, plot and characterization. And in some ways Goldsmith achieved this by accident, since he deliberately chose the familiar though limited background of his own life for his subject matter to avoid having to explore any wide range of his imagination. Yet he molded the lessons of his own nature, suffering, emotions, waywardness and disciplines into a cohesive whole, and in so doing wove a subtly **didactic** thread through the fabric of his tale. His **theme** is sparse, his characters are by no means profound, and his plot is simple, yet he has rare moments in which the **didactic** impact of his narrative is felt by all his readers.

Moral Aspects

Goldsmith establishes and maintains a strong moral tone throughout his story, in which good predominates over evil. We are taught that perseverance in the will of God, a cheerful view toward work, patience in the face of adversity, and an indulgent, forgiving attitude to the failings of others are all virtues to be obeyed and revered. Yet these virtues need not be achieved by superhuman effort, but can exist in a person side by side with vanities, weaknesses and follies. Critics sympathetic to this novel claim that Goldsmith was really trying to show us that man, on his perilous voyage through life, has a noble stature and role even in the humblest of circumstances. This argument is backed up by the prison scene in which Dr. Primrose is surrounded by sneering felons; for among these wretches the vicar finds, on a social level, a common nature to which he can appeal and depraved minds that he may be able to instruct, and in theological terms, souls that he can save. As he himself said: "In less than a fortnight I had formed them into something social and humane." We must not forget that when this was written, the famous English prison reformer, Elizabeth Fry, was not even born. In the midst of all the talk about Augustan moral order, decency, and obedience to law, prisons were at best hell-holes of squalor and disease, and at worst gateways to the gallows. Dr. Primrose's arguments against the foul penal system are quite remarkable, considering the day and age. He says that prison makes a man guilty where it finds him innocent; men are imprisoned for one petty social offense and prison releases them fully prepared and trained to commit a thousand major crimes. The reader is told, for example, that "penal laws, which are in the hands of the rich, are laid upon the poor," and that "when by indiscriminate penal laws a nation beholds the same punishment affixed to dissimilar degrees of guilt, from perceiving no distinction in the penalty, the people are led to lose all sense of distinction in the crime." These are in fact remarkable observations for someone living in a society almost totally callous to the appalling plight of prisoners and to the gross injustices of the English penal code.

Goldsmith And Fielding

Some critics have concentrated a great deal on the resemblances between Dr. Primrose and Parson Adams, the brilliantly drawn character in Henry Fielding's novel *Joseph Andrews*. There were, of course, similarities which were almost inevitable in view of the fact that both Goldsmith and Fielding shared a sense of discernment in what was good and valuable in the human character. Yet there were major differences which cannot be ignored, and which at least suggest the improbability of the theory that Goldsmith's vicar was but a copy of Parson Adams. It is highly unlikely, for example, that Dr. Primrose's "exhortation" to the prisoners would have been included in Parson Adams' saddle-bag of sermons. Mr. Adams was also prone to devouring goodly quantities of ale and roast beef, and was not averse to delivering a sound physical beating to someone who deserved it. Such excesses of taste and behavior are quite unthinkable in Goldsmith's character, with his simple piety and sense of quiet dignity. The similarities in the two characters consist in their learning, simplicity, amusing naivete, Christian purity and benevolent attitudes. Yet there is no doubt that they are individual characters; Parson Adams being based on a friend of Fielding's called Mr. Young, and the character of Dr. Primrose finding its original in Goldsmith's own father. In fact, the particular accidents of resemblance between the two are swamped by the general differences.

The Domestic Novel

The Vicar of Wakefield is a rather remarkable novel inasmuch as it is a simple work of domestic life written without the benefit of any great tradition in this type of story behind it. The age was, in fact, unprepared for such a portrait of charming domesticity, and this fact alone may well account for its eventual resounding success in England and on the Continent when it was first published. The very fact of the hero's being a simple parson, a loving parent, and a devoted husband was remarkable in that day and age; or of his wife, with her prudence, love and respect for her husband, though "at the dictates of maternal vanity counterplotting his wisest schemes"; or of their sober labor and domestic happiness. It must be admitted, however, that there are many serious faults in the novel: it is packed with improbable situations and open absurdities. Goldsmith himself said in his brief advertisement to the novel, "There are an hundred faults in this Thing," and depended for its success on the intrinsic vitality of his characters.

The Quality Of Virtue

Critics who favor *The Vicar of Wakefield* inevitably return to the basic source of the novel's enduring success and popularity, namely the quality of virtue which permeates its pages. It is not just a homely, domestic tale of bliss and familial happiness, but rather it sets out to show that the disasters and sorrows of life can cast but a temporary pall over such a pleasant and virtuous way of life. Even in his moment of direst distress, the vicar constantly reminds us that man's injustices to fellow man are of minimal importance compared to God's eternal love for humanity. The vicar's equanimity and belief in the ultimate good inevitably survive his misfortunes. Only in one memorable scene does he lose his faith temporarily. The family is gathered around the fire, listening to young Moses' opinions on various topics, and the vicar says in a mood of jollity: "Let us have one bottle more, Deborah, my life." The news of his daughter's abduction is brought, and Dr. Primrose's comment that "we shall never enjoy one hour more" is but a momentary lapse. Charity, forgiveness, and patience prevail once more, and the grandeur and simplicity of Christian heroism survive the calamities of daily life.

The Book's Reception

In spite of the acclaim it received eventually, the novel did not cause any great sensation when it was first published, and it is interesting to examine the various reactions of some contemporary journals and periodicals. The *St. James's Chronicle* did not even make a mention of its appearance. The *Monthly Review* made the following observation: "Through the whole course of our travels in the wild regions of romance, we never met with anything more difficult to characterize than the *Vicar of Wakefield*... In brief, with all its faults, there is much rational entertainment to be met with in this very singular tale." The *London Chronicle* merely announced that a new novel had been published, and that "the Editor is Dr. Goldsmith, who has affixed his name to an introductory advertisement." The *Evening Post and Chronicle* gave an outline of its plot, and quoted extracts from the novel, such as the prison scene, but neither praised nor criticized the work. None of the members of the Literary Club - except perhaps Burke - liked it at all, and Garrick openly commented that little was to be learned from it. Admiration and acceptance of the novel slowly grew, however. In seven years it went into seven editions, and was translated into several Continental languages. Perhaps the greatest tribute of the day paid to the novel was the fact that one of the greatest intellectual figures of the era, Johann Wolfgang Goethe, said that on reading *The Vicar of Wakefield*, a fresh vision and ideal of literature and life arose in his mind. And this was no temporary opinion, for much later in life Goethe said in his autobiography that Goldsmith's novel had been one of the great blessings of his life. Even at the age of eighty-one, the great German writer openly declared that reading this book had been one of the monumental events in his mental and literary development. It is sad that Goldsmith never received such tributes in his life.

VICAR OF WAKEFIELD

GENERAL PLOT OUTLINE

....

The opening scene of the novel is the village of Wakefield, set in the serenity of rural 18th Century England. The local vicar, Dr. Primrose, and his wife Deborah have six children, of whom the most important from the novel's point of view are the younger daughter Sophia, the older daughter Olivia, and the oldest son George. Both Olivia and Sophia are outstanding for their beauty. The whole family leads a quiet, respectable community life, enjoying both financial security and an honored position in local society. George falls in love with a neighbor's daughter called Arabella Wilmot, and arrangements are made for the forthcoming marriage. Unfortunately, an argument takes place between Miss Wilmot's father and Dr. Primrose over the question of monogamy. This quarrel was triggered off by the fact that Mr. Wilmot is on the brink of taking a fourth wife, which offends the vicar's sense of decency. Dr. Primrose stoutly defends his ideas on monogamy, which anger and outrage Mr. Wilmot to the extent that a wide gulf is created between the two families. At this point in the story we learn that the vicar's broker has absconded with all his funds, and this puts a definite end to the wedding plans. Dr. Primrose has not only annoyed and insulted

Mr. Wilmot, but has become impoverished, so the bride-to-be's father cancels all the arrangements.

The migration of the Primrose family now takes place following these disasters. George sets out for London to make his fortune, while the rest of the family plan to move to another part of England, where the vicar can make a living more suited to his modest circumstances. On the way to their new home, the family falls in with a gentleman called Mr. Burchell, to whom Dr. Primrose took an immediate liking because of a charitable act the newcomer did for a fellow traveler. While on the way, Sophia is thrown from her horse, falls into a stream, and is saved by Mr. Burchell. The vicar's wife Deborah is tremendously grateful to him, and assures him of the family's hospitality if he should ever choose to visit them. The Primrose family arrive at their new home, which is on the estate of a rich young man called Squire Thornhill, who has earned a reputation for showing more than an ordinary interest in the young ladies of the district. Deborah immediately decided that one of her two daughters will make an excellent match for the wealthy and eligible young squire. As it happens, Squire Thornhill is attracted toward Olivia, and as a result of the mother's deliberate planning he becomes a regular visitor at the vicar's house. Olivia, however, makes embarrassed objections to this, claiming that she finds the squire rude and forward. Meanwhile, Mr. Burchell too has been visiting the Primrose home with increasing regularity, concentrating his attentions on Sophia, who shows open satisfaction at his attentions. Mr. Burchell, however, does not meet with the vicar's approval as a potential son-in-law, since he has lost all his money, lives in relative poverty, and seems indifferent to his indigent position.

The Primrose family is visited in their home by two well-to-do ladies who awaken the interest of Sophia and Olivia with their conversations about the delights of city life. Deborah is also extremely interested to hear that these two ladies need household companions, and she suggests that her two daughters would be ideal choices for such positions. Sophia and Olivia are thoroughly agreeable to the idea of leading a sophisticated city life, although Mr. Burchell protests violently at the very proposal. Just as the two girls are prepared to set out for their new occupations in the city, however, a letter arrives informing Deborah that some anonymous person has made slanderous allegations against her daughters to the city ladies, who now refuse to consider Sophia and Olivia as household companions. Dr. and Mrs. Primrose are at first puzzled as to the possible identity of the malicious slanderer, but soon learn that the culprit was Mr. Burchell, who is ordered from their home. He leaves without displaying any indication of shame or contrition.

Meanwhile, Olivia is more and more convinced that Squire Thornhill is continually visiting her with marriage in mind, and the vicar, who is not so sure that the squire really wants to marry his daughter, suggests that she may possibly consider a local farmer, Mr. Williams, as a husband. The squire does not ask for Olivia's hand in marriage, so she consents to marry the farmer, and the wedding date is set. Olivia runs away four days before the date of the wedding, however, and Dr. Primrose learns from Squire Thornhill that Mr. Burchell abducted his daughter. Disconsolate at this terrible event, the vicar bravely sets out to find her whereabouts and bring her the help she undoubtedly needs. While searching for her, however, he falls ill and is bedridden in an inn for three weeks. When he recovers from his illness, he decides to abandon his search for his daughter and proceeds to make his way home. On his return journey he meets Arabella Wilmot, who asks for information about the vicar's son George. Dr. Primrose informs her that nothing has been heard from or about him since his departure. Squire Thornhill, who is now wooing Miss Wilmot, makes inquiries about Olivia, but of course the vicar can tell him nothing about her welfare or whereabouts. At this time, George returns to his father, poverty-stricken and dogged with bad luck. Squire Thornhill feels sorry for the boy in his plight, grants him a commission in the army, and sends him on his way again. Before George leaves, however, Arabella promises him that she will wait for him while he is away making his fortune.

After this, the vicar proceeds on his journey home. He finds his daughter Olivia in an inn, and she tells him a tale of horror. It was not Mr. Burchell with whom she had run away, but Squire Thornhill, who had seduced her after a false ceremony performed by someone posing as a priest. The unscrupulous, villainous squire had become tired of her and had deserted her. Dr. Primrose takes his daughter home, but as they draw near to their house they see it burst into flames and burn down. They lose all their worldly possessions, but at least the family is physically safe. The destitute Primrose family is helped by kindly neighbors, however, who assist them in setting up a temporary home in one of the buildings on the estate. Word is now received that Squire Thornhill is going to marry Arabella, which makes the vicar extremely indignant. His anger is increased when the squire visits him with the offer that he (the squire) is willing to find a husband for Olivia, the intention being that she can live within visiting distance of the squire. Dr. Primrose is furious and orders the villain away, whereupon Squire Thornhill demands the vicar's quarterly rent, which, of course, cannot be paid because of the disaster.

Dr. Primrose is now sent to a debtors' prison. A short time after his imprisonment, he meets his son George, who had apparently attacked the squire physically when he heard of his cruelty, and as a result had been sentenced to be hanged for attempted murder. This seems like the end of everything for Dr. Primrose, and his miseries are compounded when he learns that his daughter Sophia has been kidnapped. But in the end, virtue, honesty, and truth triumph over the forces of evil. Mr. Burchell rescues Sophia, and, to add to the general happiness, it transpires that he is not Mr. Burchell at all, but Sir William Thornhill, the squire's uncle. Squire Thornhill's deceits and crimes having been exposed, the Primrose family once more begin to regain their former happiness. George and Arabella are reunited. Olivia's sense of shame is removed when she learns that the man who had married her to the squire was not bogus at all, but was a real priest. Sophia and Sir William Thornhill get married, as do George and Arabella. Dr. Primrose is happy at last, and looks forward to a happy old age in the contemplation of his children's well-being. To make his prospects even rosier, the broker who ran away with his fortune is captured, the money is recovered, and the vicar once more finds himself a wealthy man.

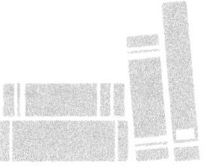

VICAR OF WAKEFIELD

TEXTUAL ANALYSIS

CHAPTERS 1 - 8

CHAPTER ONE

The story begins with the vicar's statement of his attitude toward marriage and a large family: he approves of both. We learn from the second sentence that the narrator is in orders, that is, he is a minister of the Church of England. A year after his ordination he began to think of marrying, and chose his wife, "as she did her wedding gown, not for a fine glossy surface, but such qualities as would wear well." He then goes on to describe those qualities in her which would "wear well." "She was," he observes, "a good-natured, notable woman; and, as for breeding, there were few country ladies who could show more. She could read any English book without much spelling; but for pickling, preserving, and cookery, none could excel her. She prided herself also upon being an excellent contriver in housekeeping." The narrator and his wife, according to his own reports, are quite content with their lives together, since there was nothing that could make them angry "with the world or with each other."

THE VICAR'S FAMILY AND HOME LIFE

The vicar first comments in general terms upon the kind of life he and his family lead together. They spend their lives, he tells us, "in a moral or rural amusement." In the very next phrase he more or less defines what this means: "visiting our rich neighbours, and relieving such as were poor." All of their adventures are by the fireside; they fear no revolutions and undergo no fatigues, as he puts it. Their house is elegant, situated in a fine country and a good neighborhood.

HOSPITALITY TO VISITORS

Since they live near the road, they are frequently visited by relatives and strangers. Some of these relatives, the vicar comments, did us no great honor, "For we had the blind, the maimed, and the halt amongst the number." Because most of their many guests were poor, they were usually happy with the vicar's hospitality, since, as he tells us, "the poorer the guest, the better pleased he ever is with being treated." The vicar, whose name we learn is Primrose, reveals a certain shrewdness, one might even say a certain mild cynicism, in his understanding of human nature. He has devised an unfailing scheme by which to rid himself of any troublesome guest and to make sure that such a guest will not return again. "Upon his leaving my house, I ever took care to lend him a riding-coat, or a pair of boots, or sometimes a horse of small value, and I always had the satisfaction of finding he never came back to return them. By this the house was cleared of such as we did not like."

GOOD FORTUNE AND GENERAL CONTENTMENT

Thus did the vicar and his family live for several years, in a state of what he describes as "much happiness." Dispensing hospitality and the gooseberry wine for which the vicar's household was famous, the family lived in quiet contentment; occasionally, of course, experiencing "those little rubs which Providence sends to enhance the value of its favours." The minor misfortunes, or "little rubs," as the vicar calls them, consist of his orchards being robbed by school boys and his wife's custards being plundered by the cats or the children, or the Squire's falling asleep during the most moving parts of the vicar's sermon. Occasionally too the Squire's lady would show a "mutilated courtesy" to the vicar's wife. But, we are told, the family "soon got over the uneasiness caused by such accidents, and usually, in three or four days, began to wonder how they vexed us."

THE VICAR'S CHILDREN

The vicar's six children, since they were "the offspring of temperance" and were "educated without softness," were well-formed and healthy. The sons were hardy and active, the daughters beautiful and blooming. The vicar's pride in his family is mixed with a certain amount of patriotism: "Though I had but six, I considered them as a very valuable present made to my country, and consequently looked upon it as my debtor." We are next told how at least some of the children were named. The oldest son is named George, "after his uncle, who left us ten thousand pounds." The vicar had wanted to name his first girl Grissel after her aunt, but his wife had been reading "romances" during the time of her pregnancy and insisted that she be called Olivia. He was equally determined to name his second daughter Grissel, but a rich relation wanted to be the child's godmother, and the girl was "by her directions called Sophia." All in all the vicar's family consisted of four boys and two girls. Olivia, he tells us, was a striking beauty. Sophia's features, on the other hand, were not so striking at first, "but often did more certain execution," since, as the father proudly explains, "the one vanquished by a single blow, the other by efforts successively repeated." The girls' temperaments are different and complementary. "The one entertained me with her vivacity when I was gay, the other with her sense when I was serious." Since the vicar planned to have George enter one of the learned professions, he had him educated at Oxford. The second boy, Moses, received a "sort of miscellaneous education at home" in preparation for a business career. The other two sons are not mentioned at this point in the narrative. The chapter ends with the vicar's general comment on his family: "They had but one character, that of being all equally generous, credulous, simple, and inoffensive."

Comment

Point Of View: One of the technical choices a novelist has to make in telling his story concerns what is called "point of view." This has nothing to do with the author's opinions or attitudes. It is a technical term indicating who is telling the story. There are, generally speaking, three vantage points from which a story may be narrated. There is first of all the omniscient point of view, which involves the novelist's telling the story more or less in his own voice. The omniscient author presides over the fictional world he has created as something of a deity knowing everything each of his characters knows, having equal and complete access to all of their actions and all of their inner thoughts and motives.

The omniscient author, standing outside and above his creations, not only reports their action and speech, but also describes his characters and comments on them somewhat in the fashion of an editorial writer.

Single Consciousness Point Of View: A second technical means of narrating the events of a story is one that Henry James, among others, helped to develop and perfect. It is usually referred to as "single consciousness point of view." This means that the novelist deliberately limits his omniscience, his power to see and to know everything, to the actions and thinking of one central character. Everything, in other words, is seen through the eyes of this one character. It is the novelist's voice which is still reporting the events of the book, but the scene or setting for those events is the mind or consciousness of the central character. What the author sacrifices in scope, he gains in depth of characterization of his protagonist. The single consciousness point of view is neither better nor worse than the omniscient; it is simply another way of telling a story in order to achieve different aims and effects.

First-Person Narration: Finally there is the first-person narrator, the method utilized by Goldsmith in *The Vicar of Wakefield*. In choosing this point of view, the novelist gives up his right to describe and comment in his own voice. He submerges himself totally in the consciousness and the voice of his narrator, the character he has created to tell the story in his own voice. Once again, the novelist sacrifices certain advantages by adopting this point of view, but he gains an immediacy of effect in getting us to understand and enjoy the personality and character of the person narrating the story. The emphasis, the focus, is less on the events than on the person recounting those events and on his reactions and opinions. As the title indicates, Goldsmith's chief concern is with the personality and behavior of the vicar of Wakefield. By having the vicar himself tell the story, the author achieves his artistic purpose in a directly effective manner.

The Concerns And Values Of The Novel: The opening sentence, or more accurately, the opening paragraph, helps to establish quickly the tone, the setting, and some of the chief preoccupations and themes of the novelist in telling this story. The opening sentence also suggests something of the sententious, moralistic nature of the vicar. The novel begins, "I was ever of opinion, that the honest man who married, and brought up a large family, did more service than he who continued single and only talked of population." The ethical notions of service, family and children are quickly brought to the reader's attention. We are soon made aware, furthermore, of the relationship between marriage and money. Matrimony and fortune - and their close relationship to each other - have historically been two very important institutions, or forces, or cementing agents, that have helped to keep English society organically whole and have helped to give it that special quality which it has traditionally had. It is not surprising, consequently, that the great English novels of the eighteenth and nineteenth centuries have been largely concerned with the interaction of marriage and money. One is reminded in this connection of the justly famous, brilliantly ironic opening sentence of Jane Austen's *Pride And Prejudice*, a novel which is probably the best fictional portrayal of the sociological bond between love and money. The sentence reads, "It is a truth universally acknowledged, that a single man in possession of a good fortune must be in want of a wife." In *The Vicar of Wakefield* the theme of matrimony and wealth is not fully stated until Chapter Two, but it is hinted at and foreshadowed in the first chapter.

The Worldliness Of The Vicar: Although the central character of Goldsmith's novel is officially a man of religion, an ordained minister of the Church of England, he does not reveal himself in this opening chapter as a deeply religious man. His values and concerns seem to be secular, that is, centered upon this world and upon his leading the good life. For the Reverend Primrose the good life is a blend of domestic complacency, idle gentility, rustic cultivation, and a mildly ethical notion of service to others. In many ways Goldsmith's vicar is typical of a whole breed of Anglican clergymen who in the eighteenth and nineteenth centuries led lives of quiet domesticity, undisturbed and undisturbing, often interrupting their idle leisure to dedicate themselves to harmless antiquarian studies. For such people the religious life was often defined in terms of good taste and quiet cultivation of the arts.

CHAPTER TWO

The second chapter is subtitled: "Family Misfortunes. The loss of fortune only serves to increase the pride of the worthy." This moralistic, somewhat complacent maxim standing at the head of the chapter serves not only to preserve the tone established in the first chapter; it also alerts the reader that the quiet calm of the Reverend Primrose's life is about to be shattered, at least partly.

THE VICAR'S WEALTH AND GOOD WORKS

Since the vicar is independently wealthy, he is able, he informs us somewhat sanctimoniously, to turn over the profits of his living to the orphans and widows of the clergy of the diocese. He felt, he tells the reader, a secret pleasure in doing his duty without reward. He has no curate, or assistant, so he is personally acquainted with every man in the parish. He goes about exhorting the married men to temperance and the bachelors to matrimony. The results are that in a few years, "It was a common saying, that there were three strange wants at Wakefield, a parson wanting pride, young men wanting wives, and alehouses wanting customers."

THE VICAR A STRICT MONOGAMIST

The Reverend Primrose holds strong views, amounting almost to an obsession, on the subject of marriage. He wrote several sermons to prove its happiness and he maintained that a priest of the Church of England was not allowed to take a second wife in the event of his first wife's death. He has also published some tracts in support of his views. A certain theologian, William Whiston, had held the same opinion, and had had his wife's tomb engraved with the statement that she was the only wife of William Whiston. Our vicar outdid the venerable theologian, however, since he composed a similar **epitaph** for his wife while she was still alive. In this **epitaph** he extolled her prudence, economy, and obedience till death. Then he had it elegantly framed and hung it over the fireplace.

OLDEST SON'S PLANS FOR MARRIAGE

George, upon leaving college, began to court the daughter of a neighboring clergy man who was, we learn, well off, or as the vicar puts it, "in circumstances to give her a large fortune." And since the neighboring clergyman, the Reverend Wilmot, knew that Primrose was in a position to "make a very handsome settlement" on George, he approved of the prospective match.

THE VICAR'S MODE OF LIFE

At this point the narrator informs us of the kind of easy existence he and his family lead. "We were generally awaked in the morning by music, and on fine days rode a-hunting. The hours between breakfast and dinner the ladies devoted to dress and study: they usually read a page, and then gazed at themselves in the glass, which even philosophers might own often presented the page of greatest beauty. At dinner my wife took the lead; for, as she always insisted upon carving every thing herself, it being her mother's way, she gave us, upon those occasions, the history of every dish. When we had dined, to prevent the ladies leaving us, I generally ordered the table to be removed; and sometimes, with the music master's assistance, the girls would give us a very agreeable concert. Walking out, drinking tea, country dances, and forfeits, shortened the rest of the day, without the assistance of cards, as I hated all manner of gaming, except backgammon...." This life of idle tranquility is disturbed, however, by the heated discussions and the arguments which erupt between the vicar and the Reverend Wilmot, his son's prospective father-in-law. It seems that the latter, who is contemplating taking a fourth wife - he had outlived the first three - takes exception to Primrose's views concerning only one marriage for Anglican clergymen. On the day before George was to marry Arabella Wilmot, the two clerical fathers were engaged in an acrimonious debate on the question. Suddenly the vicar was called out of the room by one of his relatives and informed that the merchant to whom the vicar had entrusted his fortune had run off with the money in order to avoid bankruptcy. The relative pleads with the vicar to drop the argument at least until the wedding has taken place, especially now that his fortunes have taken such a turn for the worse. The vicar, always a man of principle, responds quickly and vigorously, "Well, if what you tell me be true, and if I am to be a beggar, it shall never make me a rascal, or induce me to disavow my principles. I'll go this moment, and inform the company of my circumstances: and as for the argument, I even here retract my former concessions in the old gentleman's favour, nor will I allow him now to be a husband in any sense of the expression." Needless to say, Mr. Wilmot, already antagonized by the vicar's marital views, upon hearing of Primrose's sudden poverty, breaks off the match between his daughter and George Primrose. The narrator concludes the chapter with the wry comment on Wilmot, "One virtue he had in perfection, which was prudence, too often the only one that is left us at seventy-two."

Comment

One must be wary of reading into a novel attitudes and opinions which perhaps are not really there. This is particularly true when dealing with a fictional milieu and with characters and values with which the twentieth century reader may not be in complete sympathy. A contemporary reader is likely to find, for example, the vicar's mode of existence and attitude toward life somewhat alien and possibly even distasteful to him. A life spent in taking walks, drinking tea, attending country dances, and composing tracts and sermons on the subject of matrimony may strike one as strange or useless. A present-day reader may have difficulty understanding, not to mention approving, the vicar's attitude toward his wife, his children, his parishioners, and life in general. The difficulty arises, however, when we attempt to determine to what extent Oliver Goldsmith shares the vicar's outlook and to what extent he may be holding up that outlook to a gently ironic ridicule.

First-Person Narration Rules Out Direct Comment: One source of our difficulty in attempting to determine the novelist's attitude stems from the fact that every word in the narrative is the vicar's; it is his voice we constantly hear; it is his opinion alone which is presented to us. By choosing the first-person narrator point of view (see comment on chapter one), Goldsmith has deprived himself of the opportunity to comment directly on the persons and events of his story. It is undoubtedly true, furthermore, that Goldsmith shared the vicar's world view to a far greater extent than probably most contemporary readers would. Having said all of these things, however, we may still detect at least an occasional note of irony in the author's creation of his central character. It would certainly be putting it too strongly to suggest that the novelist is satirizing the Reverend Prim-rose, but it is difficult to take at face value and to approve certain aspects of the good vicar's behavior and thinking.

Gentle Irony: When, for example, in the very first page of the book we are told concerning the vicar's wife that she was a lady of outstanding breeding, we may be inclined to accept that statement without further ado. But when we discover in the very next sentence what her good breeding consists of, it is difficult to suppress a smile. "She could," we are informed, "read any English book without much spelling; but for pickling, preserving, and cookery, none could excel her." We find, furthermore, that Mr. Primrose is himself capable of irony, for his next statement is, "She prided herself also upon being an excellent contriver in housekeeping; though I could never find that we grew richer with all her contrivances." One recalls too in this connection the vicar's comment on Mr. Wilmot with which the second chapter ends: "One virtue he had in perfection, which was prudence, too often the only one that is left us at seventy-two." It is interesting to note in passing that Mr. Primrose's irony is hardly, if ever, directed against himself. Whatever irony there is in his portrayal arises out of the situations and is implicit in Goldsmith's creation of this character. One feels certain that in the incident of his wife's epitaph, for example, we are expected to regard the vicar's obsessive concern with the matrimonial question as at least slightly silly. Again let it be emphasized, however, that nothing said here in any way implies that Goldsmith disapproves of his vicar or is painting a portrait in a satirical light. It is difficult to avoid the conclusion, though, that there are at least some ironic touches in that portrait.

CHAPTER THREE

With the loss of his fortune confirmed, life for the vicar and his family now changes radically. He finds it necessary, for some reason not explained, to take up residence in another parish and to take over the management of a small farm in order to supplement his income. This chapter is given over to an account of the family's journey to their new abode.

THE VICAR CONSOLES HIS FAMILY

In a truly parson-like fashion, the vicar finds it incumbent upon him to assume the task of consoling his family in their sudden misfortune. His consolation takes the form of a sermonette. "You cannot be ignorant, my children," he tells them, "that no prudence of ours could have prevented our late misfortune; but prudence may do much in disappointing its effects." He concludes his sententious pronouncements with the statement, "Let us from this moment give up all pretensions to gentility; we have still enough left for happiness, if we are wise, and let us draw upon content for the deficiencies of fortune."

THE FAMILY LEAVES

It is found necessary to send the oldest son, George, to London, where he will be able to earn some money for himself and the rest of the family. Primrose sends him on his way with five guineas and, inevitably, a parcel of good advice. The rest of the family a few days later begin their sad journey to their new home. At the end of the first day's travel, they take lodgings at an inn. The innkeeper knows the neighborhood into which they are moving. He tells the family in particular about Squire Thornhill, who is to be the vicar's landlord. The squire, we learn, is completely devoted to a life of pleasure and is something of a rake. While conversing with his host, the vicar hears of a young man staying at the inn who is unable to pay his bill because he had given his money to the town beadle "to spare an old broken soldier, that was to be whipped through the town for dog-stealing." The vicar, moved by the tale of the young man's generosity, asks to meet him and offers to pay his bill. The stranger, whose name is Mr. Burchell, turns out to be a forthright young man, possessing a good mind and strong opinions. He journeys along the way with the vicar and his family, as Sir William Thornhill, the vicar proceeds to describe young squire's uncle, a man whose reputation the vicar knows as "one of the most generous, yet whimsical men in the kingdom; a man of consummate benevolence." Burchell replies that he was too much so, for his generosity led to a "romantic extreme." At this point their young companion tells the Primrose family all about Sir William Thornhill, launching into a full description of his excesses on the side of virtue. "The slightest distress," Burchell remarks, "whether real or fictitious, touched him to the quick, and his soul laboured under a sickly sensibility of the miseries of others." In time Thornhill had given away most of his fortune, and then instead of money he gave promises. "They were all he had to bestow, and he had not resolution enough to give any man pain by a denial. By this he drew round him crowds of dependents, whom he was sure to disappoint, yet wished to relieve." Eventually he resolved to regain his fortune "by travelling through Europe on foot," and once again he is as affluent as he had been formerly. He has given over most of his fortune to his young nephew, Squire Thornhill, to do with as he pleases. Burchell concludes his character sketch of the elder Thornhill with the observation, "At present, his bounties are more rational and moderate than before; but still he preserves the character of a humorist, and finds most pleasure in eccentric virtues."

BURCHELL TO THE RESCUE

The vicar observes of his newly found, talkative young companion, "What surprised me most was, that though he was a money borrower, he defended his opinions with as much obstinacy as if he had been my patron." Burchell, however, is more than a talker; he is a quick-thinking man of action. In the midst of their conversation the two men suddenly hear a scream, and looking in the direction from which it has come, they discover that the vicar's youngest daughter has been thrown from her horse into a rapid stream. Although she has already sunk twice, the vicar is powerless to go to her rescue quickly enough. Burchell, however, plunges in and rescues her, and the vicar observes, "Her gratitude may be more readily imagined than described; she thanked her deliverer more with looks than words, and continued to lean upon his arm, as if still willing to receive assistance." Mrs. Primrose too is attracted by the heroic young stranger, and later comments romantically to her husband that if Burchell "had birth and fortune to entitle him to match into such a family as ours, she knew no man she would sooner fix upon." On hearing this, the vicar is led to observe, "I could not but smile to hear her talk in this lofty strain: but I was never much displeased with those innocent delusions, that tend to make us more happy." An earlier edition of *The Vicar of Wakefield* contained a slightly expanded and more sharpened version of the vicar's comment. In the 1766 version Goldsmith had written, "I could not but smile to hear her talk in this strain: one almost on the verge of beggary thus to assume language of the most insulting affluence, might excite the ridicule of ill-nature." One must admit that the earlier, more pointed version, with its epigrammatic quality, seems to be a more appropriate conclusion to the chapter than the later, toned-down version.

Comment

Importance Of Money: The importance of money in the lives of these characters continues to occupy a central position in the unfolding of the story. The vicar's sudden loss of his fortune leads directly to the departure of one member of the family, George, and the move by the rest of the family to a new dwelling. As a narrative device, the vicar's impoverishment triggers a new set of episodes, is the source of a major conflict, and sets in motion a new chain of events and introduces us to a new cast of characters. The journey technique, which leads to encounters with new people and produces new adventures, is at least as old as Homer's *Odyssey*. Some other examples of this journey device include Virgil's *Aeneid*, Fielding's *Tom Jones*, and Mark Twain's *Huckleberry Finn*. Goldsmith, of course, in *The Vicar of Wakefield* does not construct his whole plot around a journey, as so many other authors have done. He merely makes use of it as a means of getting his narrative vehicle off the ground. And, as we said before, his launching device is the importance of money in his characters' lives.

Consistency Of Characterization: The vicar continues to be very much as we saw him in the first two chapters, even though the circumstances of his life have altered radically. Still possessed of his complacent good humor, he continues to be moved by slightly patronizing but generous impulses toward charitable gestures, and he goes on offering moralistic advice to those he feels to be in need of it. In addition to the general sermon he preached to his family (parts of which were quoted above), he also, somewhat after the fashion of a Polonius, paternalistically counsels his son as he sends him off to London. "You are going, my boy," he tells him, "to London, on foot, in the manner Hooker, your great ancestor, travelled there before you. Take from me the same horse that was given him by the good Bishop Jewel, this staff; and take this book too, it will be your comfort on the way: these two lines in it are worth a million: I have been young, and now am old: yet never saw I the righteous man forsaken, or his seed begging their bread.' Let this be your consolation as you travel on. Go, my boy, whatever be thy fortune, let me see thee once a year: still keep a good heart, and farewell." There is no mention of George's response.

New Characters: The reader is introduced to several new characters in this chapter. It is interesting to observe Goldsmith's skill in achieving variety in the manner of making us acquainted with these new characters. In the first place, they are not all of equal importance. The inn-keeper, for instance, is merely a functional presence. Next we hear about Squire Thornhill, but we do not meet him yet. This serves as a preparation for our encounter with this important character at a later stage of the narrative. We are given a character sketch, a vignette, of his uncle, Sir William Thornhill, by Mr. Burchell. This set-piece description by Burchell, which takes up a good part of this chapter, belongs to a genre of writing of which writers and readers in the seventeenth and eighteenth centuries seemed to have been fond. In limitation of the ancient writer Theophrastus, authors like Overbury in the seventeenth century and Addison and Steele in the eighteenth frequently wrote what were commonly called "characters." Burchell's didactic description of Thornhill belongs to the same tradition.

Burchell: Direct Characterization: In contrast to the other new characters in this chapter, Mr. Burchell is presented to us directly. We first hear about him from the innkeeper; then the vicar says a word or two about him, and finally we encounter him face to face, hear him talking and observe him acting. He is, we discover, a strong-willed, intelligent man of action, standing as an obvious contrasting foil to Squire Thornhill, whom we have not as yet met, but about whom we have heard some unpleasant facts. Goldsmith's ability to vary the ways in which he introduces his characters into the narrative is a minor but important aspect of his skill as a novelist.

CHAPTER FOUR

Chapter four is given over completely to a description of the vicar's new abode and the style of life to which he and his family quickly became accustomed. It soon becomes clear that despite the recent loss of most of their worldly fortune, the Primrose family is hardly living an impoverished existence. It is not even a question of their living in shabby gentility. Gentility yes, shabby no. They live on a beautiful, twenty-acre tract of land, in a comfortable thatched cottage, and keep a servant to attend to the more menial chores, such as lighting the fire before they all rise in the morning. Their neighbors all lead simple, comfortable lives, being "equal strangers to opulence and poverty." The community is what an anthropologist might call tradition-directed. The vicar's neighbors, he informs us, "kept up the

Christmas carol; sent true-love knots on Valentine morning; ate pancakes on Shrovetide; showed their wit on the first of April; and religiously cracked nuts on Michaelmas-eve. Being apprized of our approach, the whole neighbourhood came out to meet their minister, dressed in their fine clothes, and preceded by a pipe and tabor; a feast also was provided for our reception, at which we sat cheerfully down; and what the conversation wanted in wit was made up in laughter." The entire way of life of these people is described in terms of bucolic, pastoral simplicity. The little society is conservative, self-contained, provincial in the fullest sense of the term.

THE FAMILY'S WAY OF LIFE

Despite their move to new, humbler quarters, the Primrose family's way of life does not seem to have changed greatly. The vicar refers to the family life as "the little republic to which I gave laws." His little republic was regulated in the following manner: "By sunrise, we all assembled in our common apartment, the fire being previously kindled by the servant. After we had saluted each other with proper ceremony, for I always thought fit to keep up some mechanical forms of good breeding…we all bent in gratitude to that Being who gave us another day. This duty being performed, my son and I went to pursue our usual industry abroad, while my wife and daughters employed themselves in providing breakfast, which was always ready at a certain time. I allowed half an hour for this meal, and an hour for dinner; which time was taken up in innocent mirth between my wife and daughters, and in philosophical arguments between my son and me." More details of the family's mode of existence are given, but the brief description just quoted gives an adequate idea of the highly formalized, carefully regulated pattern of life followed by the family. Occasionally they entertained guests, serving them the gooseberry wine "for the making of which we had lost neither the receipt nor the reputation." These guests, such as the talkative farmer Flamborough and the blind piper, would often entertain the assembled company by singing traditional **ballads** such as "Johnny Armstrong's Last Good Night" and "Barbara Allen."

SUNDAY FINERY: A MINOR CRISIS

The major event of this chapter has to do with the minor crisis created by the Primrose women's decking themselves out in their most elegant finery in order to attend Sunday services. The vicar's response to their splendid adornment is to send his son out to fetch the coach to take them to the church. The women are amazed at the command, for, as Mrs. Primrose says, "Surely, my dear, you jest; we can walk it perfectly well: we want no coach to carry us now." To which the vicar replies, "You mistake, child, we do want a coach, for if we walk to church in this trim, the very children in the parish will hoot after us." He goes on to complain that their dress is characterized not by neatness but by frippery. "These rufflings, and pinkings, and patchings, will only make us hated by all the wives of all our neighbours." His complaints, he informs us, had the desired effect. "The next day I had the satisfaction of finding my daughters, at their own request, employed in cutting up their trains into Sunday waistcoats for Dick and Bill, the two little ones; and, what was still more satisfactory, the gowns seemed improved by this curtailing."

Comment

The eighteenth century had a higher tolerance for straight, unabashed didacticism in its literature than presumably most twentieth century readers do. Chapter Four of *The Vicar of Wakefield* - as well as most of the novel in fact - is a case in point. The primary purpose of this chapter is instructional, presenting as it does an idealized portrait of an idealized life, "the quiet life," as sixteenth century writers used to call it. Eighteenth century readers and writers took to heart Horace's famous dictum that literature should be both "'dulce ac utile'— useful as well as entertaining." In fact the useful or didactic aspects of a literary work provided the major source of the work's entertainment value.

The Vicar's Religious Sensibilities: It is interesting to observe that the religious values of this man of God, the Reverend Primrose, are conceived of and defined in terms of the rather vague, doctrineless theology usually associated with the eighteenth century. This religious sense, usually known as Deism, de-emphasizes dogma, stresses ethical moderation and good taste, and has little or nothing to do with historical Christianity. The god of the Deists is the god of the philosophers, and is often referred to as the "Supreme Being," the very phrase used by the vicar in describing the family's ritual of morning prayer. It is significant too that the good vicar's objections to the dress of his women folk have less to do with ethical considerations than with what some moralists refer to as human respect, that is, a concern for what people will say.

CHAPTER FIVE

The stage has now been sufficiently set for further plot complications. The vicar, his family, their way of life and their values have been sufficiently defined, and other major characters such as Burchell and Squire Thornhill have, at least to some extent, been brought to our attention. The action of this and the succeeding chapters continues to focus our attention upon the interrelationship of love, marriage, and wealth.

THE SQUIRE APPEARS

One form of recreation indulged in by the vicar and his family is to take tea in a quiet, picturesque section of their small estate. Here they passed much of their leisure time, reading, singing, strolling, and passing the time in amiable conversation. It happens that one autumn holiday while the Primrose family is assembled in this spot for its relaxation, the sounds of the hunt are heard and a frightened, panting stag comes into view. Not far behind it are the hunters, and bringing up the rear is a young gentleman "of a more genteel appearance than the rest." The stranger alights from his horse, and without waiting to be properly introduced by the vicar, immediately approaches the young ladies in the party. His name, we discover, is Thornhill, Squire Thornhill, the owner of the estate upon which the vicar and his family live. The young ladies favor their guest and landlord with a song upon the guitar. Thornhill, delighted by the performance, takes up the instrument and renders a number himself, but in a rather mediocre fashion, we are told. The elder Primrose girl, however, seems quite taken with the handsome young squire and applauds loudly. "He praised her taste, and she commended his understanding." At the approach of evening he prepares to depart, having impressed all of the family, except, of course, the vicar. Before leaving he requests permission to come back for another visit, which, the vicar wryly remarks, "as he was our landlord, was most readily agreed to."

POSSIBILITY OF MARRIAGE

Immediately after the young man's leaving, Mrs. Primrose "called a council on the conduct of the day." She is somewhat prematurely and foolishly excited at the possibility of Squire Thornhill's courting and marrying one of her daughters. Significantly, she seems most impressed by the squire's wealth, for, we learn, "She hoped again to see the day when we might hold up our heads with the best of them; and concluded, she protested she could see no reason why the two Miss Wrinklers should marry great fortunes and her children get none." Sophy at this point praises the squire's good qualities, while Olivia voices her disapproval. The vicar shrewdly comments, "These two last speeches I interpreted by contraries. I found by this, that Sophy internally despised, as much as Olivia secretly admired him."

SOME GOOD ADVICE AND A SIDE OF VENISON

The vicar, typically and predictably, now launches into a short speech, which might be labeled paternal advice to the young and innocent. "I have no apprehensions," he says, "from the conduct of my children; but I think there are some from his character." The good preacher is interrupted at this point by the arrival of one of Thornhill's servants who, with the squire's compliments, brings the Primroses a side of venison together with a promise to dine with them in a few days. This well-timed present succeeds in neutralizing all of the vicar's arguments and he relapses into silence, thinking to himself, "That virtue which requires to be ever guarded, is scarce worth the sentinel."

CHAPTER SIX

The vicar and his family agree to have some of the venison that same evening for supper. The vicar regrets that no stranger or neighbor is present to share the feast with them. Just as he is uttering these noble sentiments, who should appear but Mr. Burchell, the impoverished young rescuer of Sophia. Burchell, it seems, spends a few days in their neighborhood each year, living on the hospitality of the countryside. Mrs. Primrose announces the young man's arrival to her husband, exclaiming, "Here comes our good friend Mr. Burchell, that saved our Sophia, and that run you down fairly in the argument." The vicar does not take kindly to the latter part of his wife's statement, commenting, "Confute me in argument! child, you mistake there, my dear. I believe there are but few that can do that: I never dispute your abilities at making a goose-pie, and I beg you'll leave argument to me."

BURCHELL THE HOUSE GUEST

Mr. Burchell, the vicar informs the reader, talks at intervals with good sense, but he preferred the company of children, whom he referred to as "harmless little men." He delighted in singing them ballads, reciting stories and making presents to them of little trinkets and toys. Although there is no extra room for a guest in the Primrose home, Burchell is able to stay the night with them because the children offer to double up and give him one of their beds. The next day is spent in bringing in the hay, Burchell happily joining in the effort. As the work proceeds, the vicar observes a development which makes him somewhat uneasy: "I could not avoid...observing the assiduity of Mr. Burchell in assisting my daughter Sophia in her part of the task. When he had finished his own, he would join in hers, and enter into a close conversation."

BURCHELL LEAVES AND IS DISCUSSED

In the evening Burchell leaves to spend the night with a neighbor, whose child he had promised a whistle. The vicar ruminates aloud upon the extravagant, wasteful youth Burchell has spent - he is not yet thirty - and suggests that perhaps he deserves his poverty. Sophia in defense of the young man, gently reproves her father, "Whatsoever his former conduct may be, Papa, his circumstances should exempt him from censure now." Young Moses Primrose also comes to Burchell's defense, citing an ancient fable from Greek mythology to prove his point. Moses innocently ends his brief for the defense with the remark, "This man's mind seems fitted to his station; for I never heard any one more sprightly than he was to-day when he conversed with you." Sophy, to whom this comment is addressed, blushes and laughs affectedly. The vicar thinks to himself, "The readiness with which she undertook to vindicate herself, and her blushing, were symptoms I did not internally approve; but I repressed my suspicions."

PREPARATIONS FOR THORNHILL'S ARRIVAL

The chapter closes with a brief description of the excited preparations undertaken for the arrival of the young squire the next day. The most important of these preparations, as far as the girls are concerned, is a "wash for the face," or a cosmetic. Naturally, the vicar disapproves, since, he observes, "Instead of mending the complexion, they spoiled it." He tells us what he did to thwart the girls' plans: "I therefore approached my chair by sly degrees to the fire, and grasping the poker, as if it wanted mending, seemingly by accident, overturned the whole composition; and it was too late to begin another." The vicar, we see, is not above a sly trick or two in defense of good conduct and righteous living.

Comment

Chapters Five and Six might be regarded as companion pieces, standing in an antithetical or contrasting relationship to each other. Each is centered upon the presence of a young man, Squire Thornhill and Mr. Burchell respectively. Each of these characters seems interested in one of the vicar's daughters, Olivia and Sophia. The vicar, in turn, but for different reasons, disapproves of the attentions the two men pay to his daughters. There, however, the resemblance ends. Thornhill is a wealthy, pleasure-loving rake, while Burchell, who had formerly been prodigal of his fortune, is an earnest young man who likes ballads, young children, and Sophia. He seems, in short, to be poor but honorable. By juxtaposing these two characters, by bringing them into the narrative more or less together and contrasting them with one another, Goldsmith is able to heighten the characterization of each by playing off the qualities of one against the traits of the other. This foil technique is, of course, as old as the art of story-telling itself, but it should be noticed how skillfully the novelist employs it here.

Marriage And Fortune: It has already been observed how closely intertwined matrimony and money are in Goldsmith's novel. It is sufficient to observe here that this close relationship is sustained and deepened as the story progresses. Squire Thornhill is regarded as "a good catch" at least as much for his great wealth as for his superficial veneer of charm and good looks. Burchell, on the other hand, is judged harshly precisely because of his low financial standing in the community. Whether this standard of judgment is a vestigial remnant of an earlier interpretation of the Calvinist ethic, whereby worldly success was sometimes taken as a sign of heavenly predestination, is difficult to say. One writer on the subject, Lionel Trilling, has suggested that this emphasis upon property and wealth in the English novel is more complicated than either Calvinist ethics or the universal acquisitive instinct would suggest. Mr. Trilling argues that now that the "upper classes" have social station without a corresponding social function (such as policing or protection, as was the case with their predecessors, the medieval knights), there is now an anxious and undue emphasis upon the symbols and accoutrements of class and station. In other words, wealth as a symbol of caste or station accounts for its importance in the English social novel in the eighteenth and nineteenth centuries. It is a tantalizingly suggestive argument.

The Style Of The Novel: Not the least important quality of this work and one which undoubtedly helped to endear it to countless readers of previous generations is its style. Written in the formal, heightened prose and employing the balanced rhetoric which the eighteenth century loved so dearly, Goldsmith's novel has made its appeal to many readers as much for its manner as for its matter. And since, furthermore, the narrator of the story is an educated man trained as a preacher, it is natural and plausible that he should speak the kind of balanced rhetoric which he does. Discussing Burchell with his family in Chapter Six, for example, the vicar says, "Poor forlorn creature! where are now the revellers, the flatterers, that he could once inspire and command? Gone, perhaps, to attend the pander grown rich by his extravagance. They once praised him, and now they applaud the pander; their former raptures at his wit are now converted into sarcasms at his folly: he is poor, and perhaps deserves poverty; for he has neither the ambition to be independent, nor the skill to be useful." This combination of moral sentiment and rhetorical parallelism was revered highly by Goldsmith and his contemporaries.

The Vicar's Aphorsims: Another aspect of this stylistic taste is to be found in the vicar's affection for aphorisms, that is, brief, pithy moral statements packed into concise, epigrammatic sentences. The book is filled with them. Here are a few, taken from Chapters Five and Six: Chapter Five is subtitled aphoristically, as are many of the other chapters: "What we place most hopes upon generally proves most fatal." And again, "Disproportioned friendships ever terminate in disgust." "There is no character more contemptible than a man that is a fortune-hunter." "That virtue which requires to be ever guarded, is scarce worth the sentinel." "We should never strike one unnecessary blow at a victim over whom Providence holds the scourge of its resentment." And finally, as Moses says to his father in defense of Mr. Burchell, "We are not to judge of the feelings of others by what we might feel if in their place. However dark the habitation of the mole to our eyes, yet the animal itself finds the apartment sufficiently lightsome."

Contemporary taste may not be so closely attuned to the kind of rhetorical elegance represented by the preceding quotations. But it must be recognized that for approximately four centuries most English prose was written to satisfy such a taste.

CHAPTER SEVEN

Chapter Seven is given over to an account of Squire Thornhill's visit to the Primrose home. The chapter is subtitled: "A town wit described. The dullest fellows may learn to be comical for a night or two." The squire's witty conversation dominates this ritual occasion. After one not particularly humorous sally, the vicar reports, "At this he laughed, and so did we. The jests of the rich are ever successful." The vicar begins dinner in his usual fashion, by toasting the Church. This occasions a tirade on the part of young Thornhill against the Church and what he terms its priestcraft. "A fine girl," he cries, "is worth all the priestcraft in the creation. For what are tithes and tricks but an imposition, all a confounded imposture, and I can prove it." Young Moses Primrose takes up the challenge and invites the guest to defend his position.

THE SQUIRE AS LOGICIAN

At this point in the chapter there commences a delightful **parody** by the squire of scholastic disputation, with its logic-chopping and fine dialectical distinctions. He first inquires whether Moses wants to argue the question analogically or dialogically. "I am for managing it rationally," replies the vicar's son. Then the squire begins to establish the premises from which he will draw his conclusions: whatever is, is; a part is less than the whole; the two angles of a triangle are equal to two right ones. Then he proceeds with his fantastic argumentation. "The premises being thus settled, I proceed to observe, that the concatenation of self-existences proceeding in a reciprocal duplicate ratio, naturally produce a problematical dialogism, which in some measure proves, that the essence of spirituality may be referred to the second predicable." Moses at this point interrupts to accuse Thornhill of holding heterodox views. The squire's response is priceless: "What, not submit! Answer me one plain question: do you think Aristotle right, when he says, that relatives are related?" Moses agrees to the startling proposition. "If so, then," cries the squire, "Answer me directly to what I propose:

Whether do you judge the analytical investigation of the first part of my enthymeme deficient, secundum quoad, or quoad minus? and give me your reasons." The vicar's young son, his head spinning, is totally confounded by this versatile display of logical nonsense and double talk. Everyone, except the vicar, laughs heartily at poor Moses' discomfiture.

THE SQUIRE IS ONCE AGAIN DISCUSSED

All are agreed that the squire's attentions and affections are centered upon Olivia. Mrs. Primrose is elated. "I'll fairly own," she tells her husband, "that it was I that instructed my girls to encourage our landlord's addresses. I had always some ambition; and you now see that I was right; for who knows how this may end?" The vicar gloomily agrees with this last sentiment. His wife goes on to suggest that Olivia, should she ever marry the squire, may convert him from his free-thinking, since, she says, her oldest daughter "is very well skilled in controversy." The vicar expresses his profound doubts as to his daughter's qualifications as a religious controversialist. Olivia at this point presents her credentials as a skilled and informed debater: "I have read a great deal of controversy. I have read all the disputes between Thwackum and Square [two farcical characters in Fielding's *Tom Jones* who constantly engage in ridiculous but heated arguments]; the controversy between Robinson Crusoe and Friday the savage." Her father's ironic response to this impressive recital of qualifications closes the chapter: "Very well, that's a good girl: I find you are perfectly qualified for making converts, and so go help your mother to make the gooseberry-pie."

Comment

This chapter might be cited as evidence that Oliver Goldsmith, in creating Vicar Primrose - loosely modeled, after a fashion, on his own father - held a somewhat ambivalent attitude toward the clergyman hero of his novel. It cannot really be denied that the author obviously plunge with a certain gusto and relish into composing the humorous burlesque of logic which he puts into the mouth of Squire Thornhill. The reader - and one presumes the author as well - cannot help admiring, at least to some extent, the mad wit of the young landlord as opposed to the stuffy solemnity of the vicar's young son. The vicar does not approve of this spoofing of syllogistic reasoning, but it is fairly clear that Goldsmith does, and that he expects his readers to do so as well. Furthermore, the squire, at least so far, seems to be a rather engaging, charming young man, a person capable of captivating not only Olivia Primrose, but the discerning reader as well.

CHAPTER EIGHT

Mr. Burchell returns to the scene once again, and the vicar informs us of the displeasure with which he regards the frequency of the young man's visits. During his visit he worked hard, as usual, and his company and conversation were pleasant and entertaining. The vicar's uneasiness at Burchell's presence arose from the fact that he was obviously becoming increasingly attached to Sophia and she to him. As they are all dining out of doors, listening to two blackbirds answering each other from opposite hedges, Sophy is reminded of the two lovers in a poem by Gay who are struck dead in each other's arms. Moses answers that Ovid has done this kind of thing much better. "The Roman poet," he says, "understands the use of contrast better; and upon that figure artfully managed, all strength in the pathetic depends." (We have already observed that Goldsmith himself was fond of that literary technique.) Burchell complains that most English poetry these days is too much given over to "loading all their lines with epithet." He makes this criticism by way of introducing a **ballad** which he recites to the company. Burchell's **ballad** (composed actually by Goldsmith) is a sentimental tale of the re-uniting of two separated lovers. The hero of the poem is, like Burchell, poor but honest, and the lady, a wealthy heiress, almost loses him permanently as a result of her cruelty. The peacefulness of the moment is shattered by a nearby gunshot, at the sound of which the frightened Sophia throws herself into the arms of Burchell. The shot, it turns out, was fired by the squire's chaplain, who has shot one of the blackbirds. He makes a present of the dead blackbird to the distraught Sophy, and invites her to be his partner at a ball to be held that evening just outside the Primrose home. Sophy wants to go with Mr. Burchell, who, however, turns down the offer, since he had promised to attend a harvest supper that evening. The vicar comments, "His refusal appeared to me a little extraordinary; nor could I conceive how so sensible a girl as my youngest, could thus prefer a man of broken fortunes to one whose expectations were much greater," namely, the squire's chaplain. The chapter closes with the comment, "But as men are most capable of distinguishing merit in women, so the ladies often form the truest judgments of us. The two sexes seem placed as spies upon each other, and are furnished with different abilities, adapted for mutual inspection."

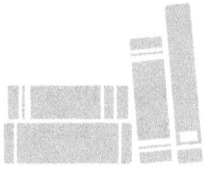

VICAR OF WAKEFIELD

TEXTUAL ANALYSIS

CHAPTERS 9 - 18

CHAPTER NINE

Squire Thornhill's presence as a major influence in the lives of the Primrose family continues to be felt, since in this chapter two new characters are introduced by the squire into the clergyman's family life. The squire and his entourage arrive at the vicar's place for the outdoor evening ball. Two of his guests are two "town ladies," Lady Blarney and Miss Carolina Wilhelmina Amelia Skeggs. They overwhelm everyone with their fashionable dress and conversation, but the vicar's oldest daughter, Olivia, is judged by everyone to be the superior dancer. During the cold supper provided by the squire after the ball, the two splendid ladies reveal a certain grossness in their conversation, but as the vicar comments, "Their finery, however, threw a veil over any grossness in their conversation...and what appeared amiss was ascribed to tiptop quality breeding." The two ladies encourage the two Primrose girls to come up to town to round out their education with the sophisticated experiences of London life. The vicar replies, "Their breeding was already superior to their fortune; and...greater refinement would only serve to make their poverty ridiculous, and give them a taste for pleasures they had no right to possess." The squire retorts, "My fortune is pretty large; love, liberty, and pleasure, are my maxims: but, curse me, if a settlement of half my estate could give my charming Olivia pleasure, it should be hers; and the only favour I would ask in return, would be to add myself to the benefit." The vicar regards this statement as dishonorable, but the squire's conversation suddenly becomes edifying, and toward the end of the evening's conversation he even asks Primrose to lead the group in evening prayers. The squire and his two lady friends ask the two Primrose girls to accompany them home, but the vicar refuses, "For which we had nothing but sullen looks and short answers the whole day ensuing."

Comment

Having sufficiently established in the early chapters of the book that the vicar and his family live a quiet life of rustic simplicity and piety, Goldsmith in these chapters is concerned to plant the seeds of conflict and build the groundwork for future complications. Before we had even met the squire, we had heard something of his reputation for seduction. The picture of his way of life, reinforced by the presence of the two town ladies, contrasts sharply with the vicar's. Goldsmith is here spinning one more variation on the ancient pastoral theme. It is an attitude adequately summarized in Rousseau's famous statement, "Cities are the graveyards of civilization." The conflict of good vs. evil is etched in terms of country vs. town, the simple vs. the sophisticated, the unadorned vs. the fashionable. It is the romantic version of the ancient conflict between appearances and reality.

It is interesting to observe, however, that as the narrative progresses, the vicar himself is more than half taken in by the wealth and splendor of the squire and his entourage. The vicar's puzzling lack of awareness is obviously dictated by the necessities of plot, for if he had from the first been completely conscious of the sinister purpose of the squire's blandishments, he would have taken steps to protect his family, and we would, consequently, have had no conflicts or complications and, therefore, no story.

CHAPTER TEN

Their flashy new acquaintances have a profound and immediate impact upon the attitudes, values and general way of life of the Primrose family. For one thing, the simple virtues of the simple life appear unsatisfactory beside the apparently splendid and exciting lives of the squire and his friends. Once again, the vicar's womenfolk become obsessed with cosmetics and beauty treatments. "The poor Miss Flamboroughs," we are told, "their former gay companions, were cast off as mean acquaintance, and the whole conversation ran upon high life, and high-lived company, with pictures, taste, Shakespeare, and the musical glasses." To complicate matters further, a gypsy fortune-teller tells Olivia and Sophia that they are to marry, respectively, a squire and a lord. The vicar too finds himself caught up in the general mood of anticipation. "We looked upon our fortunes as once more rising; and, as the whole parish asserted that the squire was in love with my daughter, she was actually so with him; for they persuaded her into the passion." The two town ladies send word that they hope to meet with the Primrose family the following Sunday at church.

A GREAT SOCIAL EVENT AND TWO STUBBORN NAGS

The vicar's wife persuades her husband that such an important social ritual must be carried out properly. She proposes that the family ride the two miles to the church on the two decrepit old plough horses that they own. Primrose offers many objections to this proposal, but, as he says, "All these objections, however, were overruled; so that I was obliged to comply." The good pastor goes on ahead of his family to the church, postpones the service for nearly an hour waiting for them to arrive, and, humiliated, finally has to begin without them. Walking home afterwards, he encounters them, "My son, my wife, and the two little ones, exalted upon one horse, and my two daughters upon the other." They had met, we learn, with "a thousand misfortunes" along the way. The horses had at first refused to move, until Mr. Burchell had beaten them forward for about two hundred yards. Next, one of the saddles had broken, and then, when that had been repaired, one of the horses had absolutely refused to move. It was at this point that the vicar met up with them. The chapter closes with his comment, "I own their present mortification did not much displease me, as it would give me many opportunities of future triumph, and teach my daughters more humility."

Comment

The events of this chapter serve to continue the conflict between appearances and reality. The reintroduction of the ladies' concerns with cosmetics and dress, a favorite butt of satirists from Juvenal down to modern times, is a concrete example of the error involved in being concerned with outward facade and veneer, as distinct from the underlying reality. The ludicrous episode with the stubborn horses is an example of the vicar's general observation made in the preceding chapter, "Greater refinement would only serve to make their poverty ridiculous." What is surprising and psychologically implausible, however, is the ease with which the ladies are able to bully the vicar into going along with their foolish plans. Previous chapters had showed us the Reverend Primrose ruling his family with a moralistic and gentle but firm hand. We have already observed that this inconsistency is the result of the necessities of plot. Goldsmith does, of course, attempt to make the vicar's actions somewhat more intelligible by showing him as blinded, to an extent, by the riches and splendor of the squire and his entourage. Primrose's complacency is, furthermore, self-righteous and fatuous, and positively inviting of further calamity. The comment with which he closes this chapter is a good example of that. It remains true, however, that there is a certain inconsistency between the vicar's domination of his family and his awareness on the one hand, and his too easy surrenders to his wife's foolish arguments on the other.

CHAPTER ELEVEN

Chapter Eleven opens with a scene of simple, rustic enjoyment. It is Michaelmas Eve (September 28) and the Primrose family is spending this ancient ritual feast visiting their neighbors, the Flamboroughs. Here the assembled company engages in the traditional festivities and games. In the midst of one of the more raucous and sprightly of these games, who should arrive but the two sophisticated ladies of the town, Lady Blarney and Miss Carolina Skeggs? As the vicar comments, "Description would but beggar, therefore it is unnecessary to describe this new mortification. Death! to be seen by ladies of such high breeding in such vulgar attitudes!" The two great ladies stay and visit, enlivening and edifying the company with their fashionably "witty" dialogue. The bulk of the chapter is given over to a recounting of their conversation. An ironically amusing note is introduced by the punctuation of each of their sallies with the contrapuntal exclamations of Mr. Burchell, who is also present. "Fudge!" he cries out intermittently as they make their points. The vicar comments, "[This was] an expression which displeased us all, and some measure damped the rising spirit of the conversation." The conversation of the great ladies gradually turns to their need for two well-educated female companions: "Of three companions I had this last half year, one of them refused to do plain work an hour in the day; another thought twenty-five guineas a year too small a salary; and I was obliged to send away the third, because I suspected an intrigue with the chaplain. Virtue, my dear Lady Blarney, virtue is worth any price; but where is that to be found?" "Fudge!" The vicar makes a quick mental computation that the two positions would pay the grand sum of fifty-six pounds five shillings, and he therefore immediately acquiesces in his wife's efforts to secure the positions for their two girls. Mrs. Primrose sings their praises and lists their accomplishments: "They can read, write, and cast accounts; they understand their needle, broadstitch, cross and change, and all manner of plain work; they can pink, point, and frill, and know some thing of music; they can do up small clothes, work upon catgut; my eldest can cut paper, and my youngest has a very pretty manner of telling fortunes upon the cards." Mr. Burchell's only response to such an amazing list of accomplishments, however, is "Fudge!" The two ladies reply that before considering the two Primrose girls for the positions, they must have references from the squire. As Miss Skeggs puts it, "Not, Madam, that I in the least suspect the young ladies' virtue, prudence, and discretion; but there is a form in these things, Madam, there is a form."

Comment

Once again the vicar's worldliness blinds him to the obvious plots and intrigues which every half-awake reader suspects to be afoot. Just as he knows the squire's reputation for seducing young maidens but still allows him to visit and charm Olivia, so too his comment in a previous chapter revealed his awareness of the essential vulgarity and crassness of the two "town ladies." And yet he agrees to a plan whereby his two daughters would be placed in the company and influence of these two questionable characters. He is completely blinded by his passion for money and by the prospect of a match between the squire and his oldest daughter. As he himself puts it, "To own a truth, I was of opinion, that two such places would fit our two daughters exactly. Besides, if the squire had any real affection for my eldest daughter, this would be the way to make her every way qualified for her fortune." The reader will notice that the vicar still doubts the squire's motives - "If the squire had any real affection for my eldest daughter" - but he nonetheless allows his wife to open negotiations with Lady Blarney and Miss Skeggs. Such blindness asks for a fall.

CHAPTER TWELVE

Upon the family's return home, Mrs. Primrose cannot contain her excitement over the momentous opportunities the future seems to hold in store for Olivia and Sophia. The vicar, however, still wanting the best of both possible worlds, hedges somewhat and makes the guarded, ambiguous comment, "Heaven grant they may be both the better for it this day three months!" He explains the cleverness of this remark in the following way: "This was one of those observations I usually made to impress my wife with an opinion of my sagacity; for if the girls succeeded, then it was a pious wish fulfilled; but if any thing unfortunate ensued, then it might be looked upon as a prophecy."

THE VICAR'S SON AS HORSE TRADER

It was now decided that the family should have a new horse to replace the old, broken-down colt they already owned. The vicar's son, Moses, who was known as a shrewd bargainer, was sent off to the fair to sell the old horse and buy a new one. He returns late in the evening without either horse or money but with a large box containing a gross of green spectacles with "silver rims." Upon inspecting them, however, the vicar discovers them to be varnished-over copper. Moses, in short, has been taken.

CHAPTER THIRTEEN

The chapter begins with Primrose preaching to his family on the folly of attempting to put on airs. He calls upon his young son, Dick, to recite a fable about the giant and the dwarf who go about seeking adventures. After three bloody fights in which they vanquish Saracens, satyrs and robbers, the dwarf has lost a leg, an eye and an arm, while the giant has come through unscathed. The dwarf refuses to fight any more battles because, as he says, "I find in every battle that you get all the honour and rewards, but all the blows fall upon me." Just as the vicar is about to moralize this fable, a dispute erupts between his wife and Burchell. The latter is trying to dissuade Mrs. Primrose from sending her daughters to the big city. She becomes so angry that she asks the guest to leave and not return. Burchell complies. The vicar upbraids his wife for her harshness, and she replies that Burchell's motive is to keep Sophia near him.

The vicar defends him, describing him as "upon some occasions the most finished gentleman I ever knew." Sophia, in reply to a question from her father, reports that Burchell once said that "he never knew a woman who could find merit in a man that seemed poor." The vicar, shifting his ground, answers, "Such, my dear, is the common cant of all the unfortunate or idle. But I hope you have been taught to judge properly of such men, and that it would be even madness to expect happiness from one who has been so very bad an economist of his own. Your mother and I have now better prospects for you. The next winter, which you will probably spend in town, will give you opportunities of making a more prudent choice." The vicar then confesses to the reader that he is not really displeased to be rid of Burchell. His conscience bothers him just a bit, but, as he observes, "The pain which conscience gives the man who has already done wrong, is soon got over."

Comment

The vicar continues to be his usual self-satisfied, self-deceiving, moralizing self. It is difficult, however, to know how much awareness he really has. For one thing, he is narrating this story from the vantage point of the present looking back into the past. This, in a sense, should give him the advantage of a certain wisdom, or at least the kind of enlightenment that one gains from seeing that one is mistaken. But Goldsmith does not allow him to have too much awareness as narrator, for this would spoil the effects the author wishes to achieve, effects of narrative suspense and characterization. Whatever discrepancy there is obviously stems from the novelist's use of the first person narrator.

Vicar Not Totally Blind To His Faults: The vicar occasionally turns his mild irony upon himself. This is what makes it difficult to determine exactly how much self-awareness this man really has. It will be recalled that in Chapter Twelve he commented on the possibility of his daughters' going to live in town, "Heaven grant they may be both the better for it this day three months!" But then he immediately observes, "This was one of those observations I usually made to impress my wife with an opinion of my sagacity; for if the girls succeeded, then it was a pious wish fulfilled; but if any thing unfortunate ensued, then it might be looked upon as a prophecy." And in Chapter Thirteen he confesses his uneasiness over Burchell's departure from his home: "Our breach of hospitality went to my conscience a little; but I quickly silenced that monitor by two or three specious reasons, which served to satisfy and reconcile me to myself." Then he concludes, typically, with an aphoristic statement of what he considers to be a moral truth: "The pain which conscience gives the man who has already done wrong, is soon got over. Conscience is a coward; and those faults it has not strength enough to prevent, it seldom has justice enough to accuse." One might conclude that Goldsmith allows the vicar a certain consciousness of his blindness and self-deception - but not too much.

CHAPTER FOURTEEN

Chapter Fourteen is given over almost entirely to an account of the vicar's visit to the fair in order to sell their remaining old horse. He too is swindled by the same confidence man, it turns out, who had bilked his son previously. He is, needless to say, humiliated, but his greatest anxiety is the prospect of facing his family. When he returns home, however, they pay little or no attention to his plight. They have just been informed that Olivia and Sophia will not be journeying to town as companions to Lady Blarney and Miss Skeggs. Someone it seems, has been spreading malicious rumors about the vicar's two daughters. The squire, who had conveyed this sad news, assures the family of his continued friendship and protection.

CHAPTER FIFTEEN

It is not long before the Primrose family discover the identity of the enemy who has been spreading false rumors about them. They find on their lawn a letter case belonging to Mr. Burchell. It contained a sealed note on which was written, "The copy of a letter to be sent to the ladies at Thornhill Castle." There ensues a brief debate over whether they should open it. The vicar is against it, but Sophia, who is sure of Burchells innocence, insists upon their reading it. The letter is a general warning against introducing "infamy and vice into retreats where peace and innocence have hitherto resided." The wording, however, is ambiguous, and the character aspersions could be taken to apply either to the two ladies to whom the note is addressed or to the vicar's daughters. The Reverend Primrose and his outraged family decide that the meaning is obvious: Burchell has infamously damaged the reputations of Olivia and Sophia. At that moment the culprit is seen heading toward their house. They decide to treat him with civility at first, so that when they do heap their indignation upon him he will feel it all the more. After some preparatory verbal sparring, the vicar confronts his guest with the evidence of his malice. Burchell readily admits the letter to be his and becomes indignant at having had his letter broken open. "Don't you know, now," he exclaims, "I could hang you all for this." The vicar's passionate anger becomes almost ungovernable at this new insolence. He banishes Burchell from their home forever, and, predictably, closes the incident by reciting a brief allegory to his family on the subjects of Guilt, Shame and Virtue.

CHAPTER SIXTEEN

This chapter is entitled: "The family use art, which is opposed with still greater." The word "art" here means skill or artifice, and the bulk of this chapter is concerned with the family's ingenuity in trying to marry off their daughter to the squire and his ingenuity in eluding them. Thornhill visits the Primrose family frequently, usually in the morning while the vicar and his son are occupied elsewhere. Primrose comments; "The hopes of having him for a son-in-law blinded us to all his imperfections."

A FAMILY PORTRAIT

They discover that their neighbors, and to some extent their rivals, the Flamboroughs, have had their portraits done by a traveling artist. Not to be outdone, the vicar and his family resolve to have a group portrait done of the whole family. The squire asks to be included, a sure sign, so they think, that he soon plans to marry into the family. The finished canvas, however, was so large that they had no place in the house to hang it. It was left, consequently, standing against the kitchen wall and became a source of amusement and the butt of jokes for their neighbors.

THE TRAP IS BAITED

Since the squire seems to be in no hurry to ask for Olivia's hand, the family resolve to pressure him into it. First the wife plans to ask his advice concerning whom her daughter should marry. Should this ruse fail to induce him to declare himself, they then plan to terrify him with a rival. The vicar is uneasy with this second plan, and yields only after Olivia assures him that she will marry whoever is chosen as the squire's rival if the latter does not himself move first. The vicar's comment is, "Such was the scheme laid, which, though I did not strenuously oppose, I did not entirely approve." They fix upon farmer Williams, one of the squire's tenants who has, in fact, already declared his interest in Olivia. When Squire Thornhill hears of this, he declares, "What! sacrifice so much beauty, and sense, and goodness, to a creature insensible of the blessing! Excuse me, I can never approve of such a piece of injustice. And I have my reasons!" He refuses to say any more, and after his departure they all discuss the meaning of the squire's statements. "Olivia considered them as instances of the most exalted passion." The vicar, however, is not so sure: "But I was not quite so sanguine; it seemed to be pretty plain, that they had more of love than matrimony in them."

Comment

Matrimony and its attendant risks, difficulties and rituals continue to be the central concern of the narrative The courtship, or the hunt, is carried on in such a way that one is never sure who is the pursuer and who the pursued. Squire Thornhill, as everyone - except the Primroses - can clearly see, is an old hand at this game, particularly when it comes to eluding capture. One is forced to conclude that it is greed alone which blinds the family to the obviously sinister nature of his designs. The vicar tries to pretend to himself that it is the fact that he is a suitor for Olivia's hand which has caused them to overlook his "imperfections." But it is clear that it is the squire's wealth which has them all dazzled. The vicar, as we have seen, once again hedges his principles in a pitiful attempt to retain his sense of righteousness and at the same time not oppose his wife's deceptions and machinations.

CHAPTER SEVENTEEN

Because of the squire's continued reluctance to propose, the vicar and his family resolve to announce the wedding of their daughter to farmer Williams one month hence. Thornhill is dejected, but as the vicar observes, "Whatever uneasiness he seemed to endure, it could easily be perceived that Olivia's anguish was still greater. As the day for the wedding approaches, the squire discontinues his visits, and the vicar finds Olivia in a state of "pensive tranquility," which he looked upon as resignation. Four days before the wedding, the family gathers around the fire in the evening, "telling stories of the past, and laying schemes for the future. The vicar's young son, Bill, sings a song taught to him by farmer Williams, "**Elegy** on the Death of a Mad Dog." It is a piece of nonsense verse, composed by Goldsmith, a variation on the old joke in which the dog dies after biting the man. This provokes a discussion between the vicar and Moses on the relative merits of different kinds of odes and elegies. The vicar declares - and here one suspects that it is the voice of Goldsmith that one is listening to: "The most vulgar **ballad** of them all generally pleases me better than the fine modern odes, and things that petrify us in a single **stanza**; productions that we at once detest and praise. Put the glass to your brother, Moses. The great fault of these elegists is, that they are in despair for griefs that give the sensible part of mankind very little pain. A lady loses her muff, her fan, or her lap-dog, and so the silly poet runs home to versify the disaster." The talk drifts on to other subjects, and the vicar lodged tranquilly in the bosom of his family and contentedly sipping wine, complacently wallows in his domestic bliss and announces to his wife, "Yes, Deborah, we are now growing old; but the evening of our life is likely to be happy. We are descended from ancestors that knew no stain, and we shall leave a good and virtuous race of children behind us. While we live they will be our support and our pleasure here, and, when we die, they will transmit our honour untainted to posterity." Precisely at this moment Dick comes running in to announce that Olivia has gone off with two gentlemen in a coach, and that one of them has kissed her and declared that he would die for her. One can imagine the impact of this blow upon the family. The vicar has been plunged from the heights of contentment into the depths of despair. His first reaction is anger and he reaches for his pistols. He is, however, dissuaded from any violent action by his wife and son. The night is spent in grief, and the next morning Mrs. Primrose declares that never again will her perfidious daughter enter her house. The vicar, however, somewhat calmed down by this time, reproaches her and seizes the opportunity to preach a sermonette on the necessity of forgiving the repentant sinner. He resolves to go out and find Olivia, saying to his son, "My son, bring hither my bible and my staff; I will pursue her wherever she is, and, though I cannot save her from shame, I may prevent the continuance of iniquity."

CHAPTER EIGHTEEN

The vicar heads for the squire's estate, and on the way is informed by a witness that Olivia was seen in a coach with a man resembling Burchell. Still unconvinced, the vicar confronts the squire, who is at home and who seems to be bewildered by the news of Olivia's running off. Another witness appears and firmly declares that the young lady in the company of Burchell has gone to a place called Wells some thirty miles away. Another tells the vicar that he has seen the two dancing the night before, "and the whole assembly seemed charmed" with his daughter's performance. The vicar immediately starts out for the place, arrives there at four in the afternoon, thinks that he sees Burchell at a distance, but the figure quickly loses himself in a crowd. He is now feverish from his emotional and physical exertions and takes a room at a small inn, where he languishes for three weeks. The vicar, who has run out of funds, is rescued by a London bookseller who had previously written some tracts defending Primrose's views on absolute monogamy for the clergy.

THE STROLLING PLAYERS

The vicar heads for home, and on the road he meets up with a strolling theatrical company's wagon. There is only one man with it since the rest of the troupe is to follow the next day. The two men strike up an acquaintance and fall into conversation. Naturally enough they discuss the present state of the theater. At the next village the two traveling companions seek shelter in the first ale house they encounter. Here they meet a well-dressed gentleman who invites them home to his house for supper.

Comment

As is frequently the case throughout the novel, Goldsmith creates many opportunities for discussing various questions of art, politics, philosophy and religion in which he is interested. These discussions are, in fact, short didactic treatises in which the novelist shares with us his own views of the question being discussed. In Chapter Eighteen, for example, the author, in the person of his mouthpiece the vicar, offers us his views of the

English drama. Since these views are more or less representative of a significant segment of eighteenth century taste, they may be of interest and deserve quoting in full. The strolling player is complaining about the current debasement of public taste: "Dryden and Rowes manner, Sir, are quite out of fashion; our taste has gone back a whole century; Fletcher, Ben Jonson, and all the plays of Shakespeare, are the only things that go down." (It is incredible but true that many men in the eighteenth century would cite an interest in Shakespeare as evidence for a decline in standards.) The vicar responds, "How is it possible the present age can be pleased with that antiquated dialect, that obsolete humour, those overcharged characters, which abound in the works you mention?" "Sir," answers his companion, "The public think nothing about dialect, or humour, or character, for that is none of their business: they only go to be amused, and find themselves happy when they can enjoy a pantomime, under the sanction of Jonson's or Shakespeare's name." "So then I suppose," returns the vicar, "that our modern dramatists are rather imitators of Shakespeare than of nature." His companion answers, "To say the truth, I don't know that they imitate any thing at all; no indeed does the public require it of them." Aside from the dubious quality of such esthetic judgments, one wonders about the propriety of introducing such a discussion into a section of the novel concerned with recounting the misfortunes of the vicar and his family.

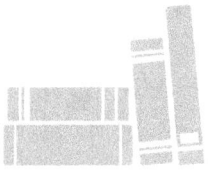

VICAR OF WAKEFIELD

TEXTUAL ANALYSIS

CHAPTERS 25 - 32

CHAPTER TWENTY-FIVE

As the vicar and his family start out on their sad journey to prison, a crowd of some fifty loyal parishioners seize the two law officers and threaten violence and bloodshed if their pastor is not released. The vicar, however, always the man of righteousness, sternly upbraids them and rescues the two officers. Arriving at the village in which the prison is situated, the vicar sees to it that his family is lodged at an inn and then he himself proceeds to his prison cell. As is the custom with new prisoners, he makes a gift of what little money he has on his person to the prisoners, who use the funds to buy liquor. The result was, in the vicar's words, "The whole prison was soon filled with riot, laughter, and profaneness," while he himself sank deeper into melancholy. The first prisoner with whom he converses turns out to be his old friend from the fair, Ephraim Jenkinson, the thief who had swindled first Moses and then the vicar himself when they sold their two horses. Jenkinson kindly offers to share his bedding with the vicar, and the latter promises to intercede with his neighbor, Mr. Flamborough, to prevent his giving evidence against Jenkinson, who in turn offers the vicar his assistance and friendship.

CHAPTER TWENTY-SIX

The vicar's family, distraught and close to despair, visits him in prison. Olivia's health has declined rapidly and seriously. To save on expenses, it is resolved that the three boys will share their father's prison cell with him for sleeping quarters. Primrose, still the paterfamilias, assigns duties to the family: "My daughter was particularly directed to watch her declining sister's health; my wife was to attend me; my little boys were to read to me; 'And as for you, my son, it is by the labour of your hands we must all hope to be supported.'s" The vicar then goes down to the common prison, where debtors and felons alike are thrown together, but here "The execrations, lewdness, and brutality, that invaded me on every side, drove me back to my apartment again." After some meditation on the subject, he decides to reform and reclaim them. Jenkinson communicates the plan to the rest of the prisoners, who received it "with the greatest good humour, as it promised to afford a new fund of entertainment to persons who had now no other resource for mirth but what could be derived from ridicule or debauchery." The vicar describes his first attempts at spiritual regeneration: "I therefore read them a portion of the service with a loud unaffected voice, and found my audience perfectly merry upon the occasion. Lewd whispers, groans of contrition burlesqued, winking, and coughing, alternately excited laughter." He then goes on to preach a sermon, after which some of the prisoners come up and shake his hand. That evening Jenkinson meets the vicar's family, all except Olivia, who remains seriously ill (and

George, of course), and he begs forgiveness of Moses for having swindled him in the sale of the green spectacles with the "silver" rims. Jenkinson seems to have learned his lesson and seems seriously interested in reforming himself. The vicar tells him the woeful tale of his misfortunes, and Jenkinson promises to see what can be done.

Comment

Jenkinson's newly found spiritual awareness and regeneration seem, at least at one point, to be influenced by a kind of debased form of Calvinism which might be summed up in the crude formula, "Honesty is the best policy." Jenkinson, for all his cunning and hard work, has wound up a poor man. As he himself puts it, "I used often to laugh at your honest, simple neighbor, Flamborough, and, one way or another, generally cheated him once a-year. Yet still the honest man went forward without suspicion, and grew rich, while I still continued tricksey and cunning, and was poor without the consolation of being honest."

CHAPTER TWENTY-SEVEN

The vicar's wife and children disapprove of his plan to reform the prisoners. He replies, "These people, however fallen, are still men, and that is a very good title to my affections…. If I can mend them I will; perhaps they will not all despise me. Perhaps I may catch up even one from the gulf, and that will be great gain; for is there upon earth a gem so precious as the human soul?" When the vicar tries for a second time to conduct a service and preach to his fellow prisoners, he is greeted with a reception of hilarity and practical joking. As he describes it, "As I was going to begin, one turned my wig awry, as if by accident, and then asked my pardon. A second, who stood at some distance, had a knack of spitting through his teeth, which fell in showers upon my book. A third would cry, 'Amen!' in such an affected tone, as gave the rest great delight. A fourth had slily picked my pocket of my spectacles. But there was one whose trick gave more universal pleasure than all the rest; for, observing the manner in which I had disposed my books on the table before me, he very dexterously displaced one of them, and put an obscene jest-book of his own in the place." The vicar, however, is not discouraged. He even begins to look into ways of bettering their temporal conditions. He found, for example, means by which each could earn a little money while in prison, "a trifle indeed, but sufficient to maintain him." He also instituted a system of rewards and punishments. His perseverance pays off for in less than six days some are penitent and all attentive. The rest of the chapter is given over to a discussion of penal reform, of common law and natural law, and a general examination of the influence of wealth upon justice in England.

Comment

This chapter is, in many ways, a prison reformer's tract. Although the vicar's efforts to "reclaim" his fellow prisoners, as he puts it, are in a sense ludicrously naive, still one must take seriously the humanitarian instincts which led Goldsmith to take an interest in this extremely important question. Goldsmith's interest in the subject of penal reform is particularly remarkable for his age. The very notion of prison as a place of rehabilitation marks Goldsmith as a thinker ahead of the consensus of his age on this question. Even now, rehabilitation is far from the actual practice of penology in the civilized countries of the world. Goldsmith's vicar, however, puts the problem succinctly and well: "It were highly to be wished, that legislative power would thus direct the law rather to reformation than severity." He objects, too, to the wide application of capital punishment for crimes of a minor nature, though he does hold that capital punishment is proper in the case of murder.

Primitivism. Goldsmith's vicar is also touched by a kind of Rousseauistic primitivism, as is evidenced in the following passages: "Savages, that are directed by natural law alone, are very tender of the lives of each other; they seldom shed blood but to retaliate former cruelty. Our Saxon ancestors, fierce as they were in war, had but few executions in times of peace; and in all commencing governments, that have the print of nature still strong upon them, scarce any crime is held capital. It is among the citizens of a refined community that penal laws, which are in the hands of the rich, are laid upon the poor. Government, while it grows older, seems to acquire the moroseness of age."

CHAPTER TWENTY-EIGHT

The vicar has now been in prison without having seen his daughter Olivia. She finally comes to see him, supported by her sister. She looks fatally ill, seems to want to die, and asks her father to comply with the squire's request. He refuses. Jenkinson also argues with the vicar, and finally advises him to contact the squire's uncle, Sir William Thornhill, a man widely known for his benevolence. The vicar agrees to this and writes to him, telling him everything that had happened. The vicar's health begins to decline, but not so rapidly as his daughter's. Reports come to him that she is dying, and finally that she is dead. He is brokenhearted that he was prevented from being with her in her last moments. He now consents to give his approval to the squire's marriage to Arabella Wilmot, but the squire scornfully rejects the vicar's message. As if things are not bad enough, his wife comes racing in "with looks of terror" to report that Sophia has been abducted by some strange men. The vicar is overwhelmed, but takes some very slight consolation in the fact that George, at least, seems to be all right, since a letter from the departed son informs them that he is well and expecting a promotion. Mrs. Primrose is relieved that George has apparently never received a letter she sent him describing all the family's misfortunes. Just then a man all bloody and fetered is brought in. The man turns out to be George, who in fact had received his mother's letter, and had immediately left his army post and challenged Squire Thornhill. The squire, however, sent four of his men instead; and in the ensuing fight George wounded one of them severely. The squire has preferred charges against the vicar's son, who now awaits the inevitable sentence of death.

CHAPTER TWENTY-NINE

Chapter Twenty-nine is the vicar's sermon, or "exhortation," as he calls it, to the prisoners. It is in the tradition of Boethius's *Consolation of Philosophy*, also written in prison, but the vicar's sermon specifically rejects philosophy as a source of comfort to the poor and miserable. There is, he says, more suffering than happiness on this earth, and man can be comforted by religion alone. The promise of an afterlife is doubly advantageous to those who are wretched, since for those who are happy "Eternity is but a single blessing, since, at most, it but increases what they already possess." For the unhappy, on the other hand, eternity "diminishes their pain here, and rewards them with heavenly bliss hereafter." Providence too is kinder to the poor than to the rich, since dying is relatively easy for the former. "These are," he tells the inmates, "the consolations which the wretched have peculiar to themselves, and in which they are above the rest of mankind; in other respects they are below them. They who would know the miseries of the poor, must see life, and endure it. To declaim on the temporal advantages they enjoy, is only repeating what none either believe or practice. The men who have the necessaries of life are not poor, and they who want them must be miserable. Yes, my friends, we must be miserable. No vain efforts of a refined imagination can soothe the wants of nature; can give elastic sweetness to the damp vapour of a dungeon, or ease to the throbbings of a broken heart. Let the philosopher, from his couch of softness, tell us we can resist all these. Alas! the effort by which we resist them is still the greatest pain! Death is slight and any man may sustain it; but torments are dreadful, and these no man can endure." The vicar concludes his sermon with the following peroration: "The time will certainly and shortly come, when we shall cease from our toil; when the luxurious great ones of the world shall no more tread us to the earth; when we shall think with pleasure on our sufferings below; when we shall be surrounded with all our friends, or such as deserved our friendship; when our bliss shall be unutterable, and still, to crown all, unending."

CHAPTER THIRTY

As George is taken off to be locked in a stronger cell, Jenkinson reports that he has heard news that Sophia has been seen in a nearby village. The jailer then rushes in to announce that she has been found, and a moment later Moses comes running in to announce that she is on her way in with "our old friend" Mr. Burchell. Shortly thereafter Sophia herself appears in person, together with Burchell, who, she relates, has heroically rescued her from her captor. The vicar asks Burchell's forgiveness for the way he has treated him, and the latter graciously pardons him. The vicar offers his daughter to Burchell, who at first remains silent and then orders dinner to be sent in for all of them.

George and Jenkinson are also invited, and when the vicar's son enters he is astonished to see Burchell and falls into a stunned, respectful silence. Burchell reproaches George for having once again done violence to someone in a duel. The vicar intercedes, explaining that his wife had sent George a letter exhorting him to avenge the wrongs done to the family by Squire Thornhill. Burchell, it turns out, is really Sir William Thornhill, the great benefactor who is known throughout the countryside for his eccentricity as well as for his benevolence. One reason for his concealing his true identity was that he wanted to see if he could discover a young lady who would love him for himself rather than for his fortune. Sophia describes her abductor, Jenkinson recognizes him from the description, and, accompanied by two officers of the prison, goes off to apprehend him since he knows where the man resides. A message to Sir William comes from the squire, who has come down to the village to see his uncle and vindicate his honor against the accusations brought against him by the vicar.

CHAPTER THIRTY-ONE

This chapter is by far the longest in the novel, and understandably so, since it is the **denouement**, the unraveling, the resolution of all of the complications of the novel. Here we find the complete reversal of all of the misfortunes, one by one, which had previously befallen the vicar and his family.

THE SQUIRE TELLS A GOOD STORY

The squire is ushered in and gives an account of his behavior which his uncle finds irreproachable. The vicar is unable to contradict any of the facts of Thornhill's version. Sir William's nephew is resolved that George should be fully prosecuted and should pay the full penalty, death, for his part in the duel. At this point Timothy Baxter, Sophia's abductor, is hauled in by Jenkinson and the two officers. Jenkinson as well as Baxter had formerly been in the employ of the squire, and their account of the squire's actions proves quite incriminating.

JENKINSON AND BAXTER TELL A BETTER STORY

Jenkinson had assisted Thornhill in procuring false licenses and false priests to officiate at the squire's many "marriages." Baxter, as he himself confesses, had been hired by the squire to kidnap Sophia in order that the latter might pretend to rescue her and thereby win her affection. Baxter is also the one who had pretended to be seriously wounded in the fight with the vicar's son, George. The squire's butler backs up their testimony. At that moment Arabella Wilmot arrives, having learned that the vicar is imprisoned in this village. She reports that her husband-to-be, Squire Thornhill, had told her that George had married and gone off to America. She is given a full account of Thornhill's villainy, but the latter retorts by saying that even if the marriage to Arabella is broken off, he still has the legal rights to Arabella's considerable fortune. Jenkinson intervenes at this point to observe that since the squire is already legally married, he has no right to Arabella's wealth. Jenkinson goes off to produce Thornhill's legal wife, who turns out to be none other than Olivia, whom the vicar had supposed dead. For the marriage ceremony between the squire and Olivia, Jenkinson had procured a genuine license and a genuine priest, unknown to his employer. He had told the vicar, with Mrs. Primrose's consent, that Olivia was dead in order that the vicar would relent, succumb to the squire's demand for an approval of his marriage to Arabella, and thus free himself and his family from imprisonment. A match is arranged on the spot-between the two long-separated lovers, George and Arabella. Sir William offers Jenkinson and five hundred pounds to Sophia, who, horrified, turns down the offer. Since she refuses the proposal, he says, he must take her in marriage himself. The vicar and his son are released from prison, the squire is stripped of his fortune and retinue, and everyone except Squire Thornhill repairs to a nearby inn for a sumptuous dinner.

CHAPTER THIRTY-TWO

All that remains for the reversal of fortunes to be complete is the restoration of the vicar's money, which had been stolen from him earlier in the narrative. This piece of business, needless to say, is quickly disposed of right at the beginning of this, the last chapter. The entire company, looking forward to the double wedding about to be celebrated, is boisterously happy, so much so that they arouse the solemn vicar's indignation. As he reports his reaction to their gaiety, "I told them of the grave, becoming, and sublime deportment they should assume upon this mystical occasion, and read them two homilies and a thesis of my own composing, in order to prepare them. Yet they still seemed perfectly refractory and ungovernable." A dilemma arises in church over which couple is to be married first, each lady wishing to defer to the other. The vicar growing tired of the discussion, interrupts, "I perceive that none of you have a mind to be married; and I think we had as good go back again, for I suppose there will be no business done here today." This, as he puts it, "reduced them to reason," and Sir William and Sophia are first married, followed by George and Arabella. The wedding feast is a time of great joy for all. The Flamboroughs have been sent for, and Jenkinson escorts one of the young ladies and Moses the other. The vicar's second oldest son, in fact, seems quite smitten by the young Miss Flamborough, and the vicar hints that a future wedding seems in prospect there. Restored to health, wealth and happiness, the vicar has nothing left to wish for. He closes the story with the comment, "I had nothing now on this side of the grave to wish for; all my cares were over; my pleasure was unspeakable. It now only remained that my gratitude in good fortune should exceed my former submission in adversity."

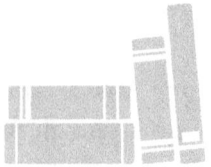

VICAR OF WAKEFIELD

CHARACTER ANALYSES

In many respects it is rather difficult to give a detailed and penetrating analysis of the characters in Oliver Goldsmith's novel, because of their lack of individual identity. On the whole they are surface sketches of set-piece types rather than involved characterizations of unique personalities. This novel is best viewed at a distance, and the reader should enjoy its best features with a certain detached attitude. If he sets out, however, to find complex profundities and psychological nuances in the character of Sophia or Solomon Flamborough, for example, he will be more than a little disappointed. Squire Thornhill is no Raskolnikov, and Deborah is no Emma Bovary. We must not castigate Goldsmith too severely, however, since he was a victim of much of the shallowness associated with Augustan sensibility, and had no great tradition of novel-writing to draw on. There are, nevertheless, some interesting features to the vicar himself, made more interesting by the fact that he is the narrator. In the hands of even the most expert novelist, the "first person" technique is a dangerous one to employ for several reasons: unless the character concerned has an extremely captivating, complicated or introspective personality, the tale lapses quickly into tedium; we do not get a clear picture of the character traits or motivations of the other personalities unless the narrator is someone of articulate perception; and finally, the author has to manipulate his narration very skillfully indeed to let the reader know, for example, whether he himself is being ironical in his portrayal of the character. Bearing these facts in mind, therefore, the student should enjoy this novel pretty much on its face value, without expecting too much intricacy of characterization. Most of the people in the tale are, as we have already said, "set-piece" or "stock" characters.

Dr. Charles Primrose

Since he is in fact the narrator of the story, we do learn more about him than we do about the other characters. On one level, he is what we would expect to find in the "typical" 18th Century English country parson. As "a priest, a husbandman, and the father of a family," he is from one angle an exemplary figure. He is kind, generous-minded, and holds firmly onto staunch views concerning Christian morality. His ideas on monogamy, for example, contain the thunder of puritanically righteous indignation, and the reader can either regard him highly for this obdurate stand or view him as a rather absurdly stupid bigot. This is one of the scenes, for example, where Goldsmith could conceivably be lampooning the whole conception of Augustan clerical piety. But since it is written in the first person, there is really no sure way of knowing. He has developed a kind of homespun philosophy, which expresses itself in his admonishing his wife and daughters for their vanity. Even here there is some inconsistency, since the portrait of the kindly, gentle, and sympathetic father is not quite in keeping with the man who assails his daughters for the "frippery" of their dress. He is fond of delivering homilies on temperance, virtue, and forthrightness, and in this respect he is again drawn as the typical country parson. On the other hand, he often strikes rather a ludicrous figure, a kind of good-natured fool easily duped by villains, and this side of his character is not quite in keeping with the man of religious wisdom we are presented with elsewhere. Also, for a man who continually propounds the eternal joys and rewards of leading a humble, Christian life, he shows a remarkably inconsistent interest in money and worldly comforts on certain occasions. His concentration on the material aspects of his daughters' marriage prospects, for example, or his glow of well-being at the restitution of his fortune, does not seem quite in line with his quietly insistent views on Christian simplicity and humility. There is also an almost **epic** quality to the heroic fortitude he displays in the face of calamity, which makes us wonder whether Goldsmith was not adopting a somewhat tongue-in-cheek attitude at the end of the novel. Yet we must not fall into the trap of regarding his portrayal with too much scepticism. He is really a character to be enjoyed as a good, lovable man, prone to gullibility, and blighted with a normal share of human foibles.

George

This is the vicar's oldest son, who is Oxford-educated and has tried his hand - and failed - at various occupations. This is the character in the novel who most closely resembles Goldsmith himself, whose opening comments on his long description of the misfortunes he had suffered on the Continent are painfully autobiographical: "...The less kind I found fortune at one time, the more I expected from her another, and being now at the bottom of her wheel, every new revolution might lift, but could not depress me." When Goldsmith describes George as a "light-hearted vagabond," he is really talking of himself.

Deborah

The vicar's wife is in one way a good person, a faithful wife and a devoted mother. In another way, however, she displays unscrupulous, ambitious, and even cunning traits which suggest that she is not merely the idyllic paragon of Augustan matronly virtues. Her main interest seems to be in getting her daughters well married, and she is quite willing to use some rather unorthodox methods to achieve this goal. She has an uncommon share of vanity in her character, and there is a touch of callousness in the revenge she seeks for the "dastardly" crime committed against her daughter Olivia.

Olivia (Livy)

The vicar's oldest daughter is uncommonly beautiful, with a coquettish, appealing personality. She shows deep remorse after her deception by Squire Thornhill, especially when she discovers that her wedding is apparently invalid. There is something unnatural, however, about the way she offers to forgive her seducer if he reforms. Goldsmith was here very obviously straining his happy ending to its limits.

Sophia (Sophy)

She is of a more modest and quietly appealing character than Olivia. A sense of her beauty and her finer qualities seems to grow on the reader as the novel progresses.

Mr. Burchell

This character, who is in reality Sir William Thornhill, is extremely generous, with a whimsical nature and humorously eccentric disposition. He is a perceptive judge of people and likes children. He shows his quality as a person by helping the Primrose family from time to time before revealing his true identity. His marriage to Sophia finally establishes the all-round familial happiness.

Squire Thornhill

Handsome, unscrupulous, and lecherous, the vicar's landlord is a villain straight out of some old melodrama. He commits a whole series of despicable crimes, but is fortuitously exposed before he can succeed in bringing down total ruin on the Primrose family and marrying Arabella to get control of her fortune.

Arabella Wilmot

Daughter of a local clergyman, she plans to marry the villainous squire after George leaves home. She is an innocent victim of the squire's wiles, however, since he has convinced her that George is married and living in America. She is undeceived in the nick of time.

Moses

He is the fourth child of the Primrose family. His is extremely naive, talks too much, and has many of his father's gullible traits

Solomon Flamborough

He is a neighbor of the Primrose family. He is extremely garrulous and repetitious, and one of his daughters is the object of Moses' affections.

Ephraim Jenkinson

This is a crafty character who poses as a venerable, erudite old man. Having duped Moses and the vicar, he later meets Dr. Primrose in jail. He tricks the squire by getting an authentic priest to marry him and Olivia.

Mr. Symmonds

This is the inn-keeper who first tells the vicar about Squire Thornhill's disreputable character.

VICAR OF WAKEFIELD

CRITICAL COMMENTARY

OLIVER GOLDSMITH

In the "Advertisement" which prefaces *The Vicar of Wakefield*, Goldsmith has the following to say about his own novel: "There are an hundred faults in this Thing, and an hundred things might be said to prove them beauties. But it is needless. A book may be amusing with numerous errors, or it may be very dull without a single ababsurdity. The hero of this piece unites in himself the three greatest characters upon earth; he is a priest, an husbandman, and the father of a family. He is drawn as ready to teach and ready to obey, as simple in affluence and majestic in adversity. In this age of opulence and refinement whom can such a character please? Such as are fond of high life will turn with disdain from the simplicity of his country fireside. Such as mistake ribaldry for humour will find no wit in his harmless conversation; and such as have been taught to deride religion will laugh at one whose chief stores of comfort are drawn from futurity."

DR. SAMUEL JOHNSON

(18th Century.) Dr. Johnson wrote the epitaph inscribed on the tablet beneath Goldsmith's bust in Westminister Abbey. It is written in Latin, and the following is the translation of the opening lines, quoted from Crocker's edition of Boswell's Johnson:

Of Oliver Goldsmith

A Poet, Naturalist, and Historian

Who left scarce any style of writing untouched,

And touched nothing that he did not adorn;

Of all the passions,

Whether smiles were to be moved or tears,

A powerful yet gentle master;

In genius, sublime, vivid, versatile,

In style, elevated, clear, elegant.

Despite these words of adulation, it should be pointed out that Johnson took very little interest in *The Vicar of Wakefield* when it was written, apart from helping to get it sold to a publisher.

BRIGHT NOTES STUDY GUIDE

DAVID GARRICK

(18th Century.) In his humorously Impromptu **Epitaph** on Goldsmith, Mr. Garrick said:

> "Here lies Nolly Goldsmith, for shortness called Noll,
> Who wrote like an angel, and talk'd like poor Poll."

Concerning *The Vicar of Wakefield*, Garrick said that there was little to be learned from it.

HORACE WALPOLE:

(18th Century.) Mr. Walpole said of Goldsmith: "He is an inspired idiot."

JOHANN WOLFGANG GOETHE

(18th and 19th Centuries.) Goethe first read Goldsmith's novel when he was a student, and said that it opened up a new world of ideas to him. Some of the main appeals in the work for Goethe were the idea that strength of will and character can overcome circumstances, and that there is a spiritual wisdom that can rise above everything and take possession of a poetical world. At the age of eighty-one he told a friend that he had recently "read the charming book again from beginning to end, not a little affected by the lovely recollection" of how much he owed Goldsmith for the inspiration he had received from his novel many years earlier. In a letter to Zelter in 1830, Goethe said: "It is not to be described the effect that Goldsmith's *Vicar* had upon me, just at the critical moment of mental development. That lofty and benevolent **irony**, that fair and indulgent view of all infirmities and faults, that meekness under all calamities, that equanimity under all changes and chances, and the whole train of kindred virtues, whatever names they bear, proved my best education; and in the end, these are the thoughts and feelings which have reclaimed us from all the errors of life."

THOMAS BABINGTON MACAULAY

(19th Century.) Macaulay said in his *Biographical Essays* that this novel was "likely to last as long as our language.... It wants not merely that probability which ought to be found in a tale of common English life, but that consistency which ought to be found even in the wildest fiction about witches, giants, and fairies. But the earlier chapters have all the sweetness of pastoral poetry, together with all the vivacity of comedy."

SIR WALTER SCOTT

(19th Century.) Scott said that "we read *The Vicar of Wakefield* in youth and in age. We return to it again and again, and bless the memory of an author who contrives so well to reconcile us to human nature."

WASHINGTON IRVING

(19th Century.) Irving adopted a totally sympathetic attitude to the novel. Speaking of Goldsmith's scenes and characters as depicted in *The Vicar of Wakefield*, Irving says that the author "has given them as seen through the medium of his own indulgent eye, and has set them forth with the colourings of his good head and heart."

WILLIAM MAKEPEACE THACKERAY

(19th Century.) Thackeray said of Goldsmith: "Who of the millions whom he has amused, does not love him? To be the most beloved of English writers, what a title that is for a man!"

JOHN FORSTER

(19th Century.) Forster, in *The Life and Times of Oliver Goldsmith*, says of *The Vicar of Wakefield*: "No book upon record has obtained a wider popularity than *The Vicar of Wakefield*, and none is more likely to endure. One who, on the day of its appearance, had not left the nursery, but who grew to be a popular poet and a man of fine wit, and who happily still survives with the experience of the seventy years over which his pleasure of memory extend, remarked lately to the present writer that of all the books which, through the fitful changes of three generations, he had seen rise and fall, the charm of *The Vicar of Wakefield* had alone continued as at first; and, could he revisit the world after an interval of many more generations, he should as surely look to find it undiminished. Such is the reward of simplicity and truth, and of not overstepping the modesty of nature."

FORD MADOX FORD

(20th Century.) Ford has this to say in *The March of Literature*: "*The Vicar of Wakefield* is a masterpiece, always with a tear of benevolence in one corner of its eye that would disgrace any other nation or any other time. In spite of the fact that (Goldsmith) covered half of Europe, supporting himself by playing on the flute, *The Vicar of Wakefield* is as far from displaying any knowledge of near-modern life as is, more warrantably, *Robinson Crusoe*. In place of displaying any sense whatever of invention, its plot is a rehash of the plots of every novelist who had preceded him, and the Vicar himself, the narrator the story, is an impossible monster. He displays at once an eminently deleterious reliance on the material efficacy of prayer and a sheer materialism that is really horrifying." Ford goes on to deplore Dr. Primrose's "implicit and unshakable belief that gilding, furnishing and material resources are the reward of the Christian virtues; that troops of servants are the hallmark of genius, and that though when you see God you die, if you can fall at the feet of a Lord - or a hero of industry - you will, if he raises you to your feet, find yourself an inmate of the home of the Christian saints here on earth. It is a point of view that must make the angels weep."

BORIS FORD

(20th Century.) In his essay on Goldsmith, Ford says of Goldsmith's prose style: "The basis of Goldsmith's distinction as a writer is his straight-forward simplicity and the unassuming elegance of his style. These qualities, though they may have come to him easily, were none the less cultivated quite deliberately. His Enquiry ends with a clear statement of his beliefs on the nature of good writing:

> **'As our gentlemen writers have it therefore so much in their power to lead the taste of the time, they may now part with the inflated style that has for some years been looked upon as fine writing, and which every young writer is now obliged to adopt, if he chooses to be read. They may now dispense with the loaded epithet, and dressing up of trifles with dignity. For to use an obvious instance, it is not those who make the greatest noise with their wares in the**

streets, that have the most to sell. Let us, instead of writing finely, try to write naturally; not hunt after lofty expressions to deliver mean ideas; nor be forever gaping, when we only mean to deliver a whisper.'

"This could have been written in no other age than Goldsmith's: it has the easy deportment that bespeaks the Augustan virtues."

VICAR OF WAKEFIELD

ESSAY QUESTIONS AND ANSWERS

....

Question: Comment upon Goldsmith's frequent reliance upon coincidence as a narrative technique in *The Vicar of Wakefield*.

Answer: The use of coincidence by a story-teller is, we must remember, nothing more nor less than a literary **convention**, that is, an agreed-upon means for economically organizing, shaping, and highlighting fictional material. **Convention** has been defined as a tacit agreement between author and reader whereby certain liberties are granted to the author, certain rights to depart from the strict observance of everyday actuality in order to heighten the effects of the story. To put it another way, it is an agreed-upon distortion of strict **realism** for literary or aesthetic purposes. Now, although coincidence is certainly part and parcel of even an ordinary human existence, the heavy reliance upon it by writers of fiction has come to be accepted as something of a **convention**. One of the world's outstanding novelists, Fyodor Dostoevski, was not reluctant to make frequent use of the device of coincidence in his novels. It is a convenient, handy way by which the novelist can bring his characters together quickly, and without a great deal of cumbersome arrangement and explanation. It is, if you like, the novelist's shorthand. A possible problem arises, however, when a novelist relies too heavily and frequently upon this **convention** for purposes of moving his story along. It can be argued that Goldsmith has done just that in his novel. He acknowledges as much when, in Chapter Thirty-one, where he relies a great deal on coincidence to bring his characters together and to reverse the downward spiralling of the plot, he pauses in his quick relation of the events to make the following explanation: "Nor can I go on without a reflection on those accidental meetings, which, though they happen every day, seldom excite our surprise, but upon some extraordinary occasion. To what a fortuitous concurrence do we not owe every pleasure and convenience of our lives. How many seeming accidents must unite before we can be clothed or fed. The peasant must be disposed to labour, the shower must fall, the wind fill the merchant's sail, or numbers must want the usual supply." An over-reliance on coincidence may very well be one of the "hundred faults in this Thing" which Goldsmith refers to in the preface to his novel.

Question: Discuss the structure of *The Vicar of Wakefield*.

Answer: The structure of the plot in this novel is a relatively simple one. The earlier chapters of the book are dedicated to defining and establishing the contented, leisurely life led by the vicar and his family. It is from these heights that the vicar will fall, gradually at first, but then the misfortunes begin to pile up more and more rapidly, until in Chapter Twenty-eight they come with such relentless rapidity that the reader is hardly able to absorb them. This represents the low point of the vicar's fortunes. Chapter Twenty-nine, the sermon to the prisoners, represents an interlude, a plateau of quiet resignation, before the vicar and his family are, with he same dizzying speed, restored in the concluding chapters to their previous prosperity and happiness, and then some. The structure of the story has been compared, with good reason, to the Book of Job.

Although several of the characters go off in different directions (George and Olivia, for example), the story line remains simple or singular rather than multiple, such as one finds in the plot of Spenser's *Faerie Queene*. The reason for this is Goldsmith's use of the first-person narrator. It is always the vicar's version of the story that we hear, which means that he must always be present at the events he narrates. We do not have a novel, then, in which the author breaks his plot line into several sections and moves back and forth from one section to another. It is only the omniscient author who can do that. The point of view, consequently, namely first-person narration, determines to some extent the structure of this novel.

Question: What are the ingredients of the vicar's world view? What do we learn of his values-religious, ethical, political, esthetic?

Answer: The vicar's religious commitment seems to be strongly influenced by the deism which characterized, generally speaking, the eighteenth century religious consciousness in England. Deism was a somewhat watered-down version of Christianity, which made little or no mention of Christ, except to admire him as an ethically good man. The deists' concept of the godhead was theologically imprecise and their religion was doctrinally vague. Deistic dogma involved not much more than a belief in a supreme being, in the necessity for living an ethically good life, and in the immortality of the soul. This seems to sum up fairly adequately the vicar's religious beliefs. Evidence for this is interspersed throughout the novel, particularly in the vicar's sermon to the prisoners in Chapter Twenty-nine.

Many of the vicar's values and beliefs can be summed up in the terms primitivism, pastoralism, romanticism. Theoretically, at least, he is distrustful of the wealthy and powerful, and exalts the simple rustic over and above the sophisticated urban dweller. He is a stout defender of monarchy, but believes in the equality of all men. His literary tastes run to the simple, the pastoral, the pietistic. The quiet, simple, domestic virtues represent to him the summum bonum, the essense of the good life. The man who wrote *The Deserted Village* is clearly the same man who wrote *The Vicar of Wakefield*.

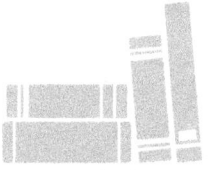

BIBLIOGRAPHY

THE SOCIAL AND ECONOMIC BACKGROUND

Allen, R.J., *The Clubs of Augustan London*, 1933.

Allen, R.J., *Life in Eighteenth-Century England*, 1941.

Besant, W., *London in the Eighteenth Century*, 1902.

Chancellor, E.B., *The Eighteenth Century in London*, 1920.

Collins, A.S., *Authorship in the Days of Johnson*, 1928.

George, M.D. (ed.), *England in Johnson's Day*, 1928.

George, M.D., *English Social Life in the Eighteenth Century*, 1923.

Mead, W.E., *The Grand Tour in the Eighteenth Century*, 1914.

Timbs, J., *Club and Club Life in London*, 1872.

Turberville, A.S., *English Men and Manners in the Eighteenth Century*, 1926.

BRIGHT NOTES STUDY GUIDE

PHILOSOPHY, RELIGION, AND EDUCATION

Abbey, C.J. and Overton, J.H., *The English Church in the Eighteenth Century*, 1878-96.

Clarke, W.K.L., *Eighteenth Century Piety*, 1944.

Cragg, G.R., *From Puritanism to the Age of Reason*, 1950.

Creed, J.M. and Smith, J.S.B. (eds.), *Religious Thought in the Eighteenth Century*, 1934.

Hearnshaw, F.J.C. (ed.), *The Social and Political Ideas of the Augustan Age*, 1928.

Hunt, J., *Religious Thought in England*, Vols. II and III, 1871-73.

Knox, R.A., *Enthusiasm. A Chapter in the History of Religion*, 1950.

Smith, P., *A History of Modern Culture*, Vol. II, 1934.

Stephen, Sir L., *History of English Thought in the Eighteenth Century*, 1876-80.

Willey, B., *The Eighteenth Century Background*, 1940.

GENERAL STUDIES

Butt, J., *The Augustan Age*, 1950.

Elton, O., *The Augustan Ages*, 1899.

Elton, O., *A Survey of English Literature*, 1928.

Gosse, Sir E., *History of Eighteenth Century Literature*, 1889.

Humphreys, A.R., *The Augustan World. Life and Letters in Eighteenth-Century England*, 1954.

Legouis, E. and Cazamian, L., *A History of English Literature*, 1935.

McCutcheon, R.P., *Eighteenth-Century English Literature*, 1950.

Saintsbury, G., *The Peace of the Augustans*, 1916.

Stephen, Sir L., *English Literature and Society in the Eighteenth Century*, 1904.

Ward, Sir A.W. and Waller, A.R. (eds.), *The Cambridge History of English Literature*, Vols. VIII-XI, 1912-14.

THE NOVEL AND PROSE

Baker, EA.., *The History of the English Novel*, Vols. III-V, 1929-30.

Birkhead, E., "Sentiment and Sensibility in the Eighteenth-Century Novel" in *Essays and Studies*, Vol. XI, 1925.

Cross, W.L., *The Development of the English Novel*, 1899.

Foster, J.R., *History of the Pre-Romantic Novel*, 1949.

Kettle, A., *An Introduction to the English Novel*, Vol. I, 1951.

Leavis, Q.D., *Fiction and the Reading Public*, 1932.

Raleigh, Sir W., *The English Novel*, 1894; rev. 1929.

Saintsbury, G., *The English Novel*, 1913.

Sutherland, J.R., "Some Aspects of Eighteenth Century Prose" in *Essays on the Eighteenth Century Presented to David Nichol Smith*, 1945.

Walker, H., *The English Essay and Essayists*, 1915.

OLIVER GOLDSMITH

Dobson, A. (ed.), *Oliver Goldsmith*, 1883.

Dobson, A., *The Life of Oliver Goldsmith*, 1888.

Doughty, O. (ed.), *The Vicar of Wakefield*, 1928.

Forster, J., *The Life and Times of Oliver Goldsmith*, Vols. I-II 1854 and 1892; rev. ed., 1905.

Freeman, W., *Oliver Goldsmith*, 1951.

Gwynn, S., *Oliver Goldsmith*, 1935.

Irving, W., *The Life of Oliver Goldsmith*, 1844.

Johnson, S., *Memoirs of Dr. Goldsmith, M.B.* (used as preface to early editions of *The Vicar of Wakefield*).

Macaulay, T.B., *Goldsmith* (written for *The Encyclopedia Britannica*, reprinted in his *Essays*).

Scott, T., *Oliver Goldsmith, Bibliographically and Biographically Considered*, 1928.

www.ingramcontent.com/pod-product-compliance
Lightning Source LLC
LaVergne TN
LVHW011717060526
838200LV00051B/2932